Series one

GHOST OF SEMINARY PAST

By

Rev. Dr. Awele Ilobah, Dish (Ed), LLB (Law), MA. (HRM), MA. (DIV), DMIN.

Reflective Theology

This publication contains the opinions and ideas of its author. It is intended to provide helpful and informative material on the subjects addressed in the publication. The author and publisher specifically disclaim all responsibility for any liability, loss, or risk, personal or otherwise, which is incurred as a consequence, directly or indirectly, of the use and application of any of the contents of this book.

JDM International Ministry
Apt 710, 2285 The College Way
Mississauga Ontario,
L5L 2M3, Canada.

Website: jdmonline.org
Hotline: *+234-802-342-5457*
　　　　+1(437)922-3236
Email:　jdmonlineorg@gmail.com
　　　　Or ilobahe4@gmail.com

Ordering Information:
Quantity sales. Special discounts are available on quantity purchases by corporations, associations, and others. For details, contact the publisher at the address above or visit our online store.

9 781736 147191

Library of Congress Control Number: IN-PROCESS ISBN-13: 000-0-00000-000-0
Paperback Edition:　　　　　　　000-0-00000-000-0
Digital Edition:　　　　　　　　Rev. date: 11/25/2020

DEDICATION

I dedicate this book to my beloved mother Sis. Ngozi Peters, whom I came into this world to know as a woman that is passionate about God and about humanity. While growing up, I was looking up to her boldness as one of the first females in ministry in my country, and early enough, she identified God's calling in my life and gave a lot of daily sacrifices and commitment to raise me to become the woman of God I am today. I am always thankful to you mummy and I am ever grateful to God for sending me into this world through you, and for all the love and encouragement and prayers and the way you stood by me through my calling in ministry. Also, I dedicate this work to my late father for the wonderful things he did in my life; to my beloved brother Joe Ilobah for his motivation and encouragement throughout the writing of this book; to My Ministry sister in the Lord Comfort Omo for your ceaseless support. Finally, to my friend, mentor, and man whom I call my educational Dad, Dr Stiver Dan, thank you for inspiring me to share the experiences of my faith walk within the African context! And for celebrating and fanning many gifts of the Holy Spirit; it raises a bubbly joyous song within my soul. I am eternally grateful to all of you.

Table of Contents

1.1 PREFACE

The Ghost of Seminary Past is a unique and uncommon book that was inspired by my many years of seminary experience. As a missionary called unto the gospel to preach the good news, I do believe that when it has to do with preaching the good news such a task comes with teaching the scripture. And to be a good teacher you must first become an apprentice or what we call a student of the trade. I see this in the Old Testament in the relationship between Elijah and Elisha; the old prophet took the young prophet Elisha under his wing and taught him the art of the trade and in the end, after he has finished training with Elisha his student, the later was hooded by the same robe that his master Elijah used. We can see this in the narrative of Elisha succeeding Elijah, 2 Kings 2:9-12.

"When they had crossed, Elijah said to Elisha, 'Tell me what I may do for you, before I am taken from you.' Elisha said, 'Please let me inherit a double share of your spirit.' He responded, 'You have asked a hard thing; yet, if you see me as I am being taken from you, it will be granted you; if not, it will not.' As they continued walking and talking, a chariot of fire and horses of fire separated the two of them, and Elijah ascended in a whirlwind into heaven. Elisha kept watching and crying out, 'Father, father! The chariots of Israel and its horsemen!' But when he could no longer see him, he grasped his own clothes and tore them in two pieces."

In the conversation, we notice how Elijah told Elisha his student, "You will receive the power and grace of a prophet if you see me being taken away from you." Christological to see means if you can comprehend the spiritual things of heaven or another way to put it may mean if you can understand the deeper meaning of heavenly things. Elijah made this comment because it is in seeking deeper things about God that a person comes to find their gifted and their calling in ministry or in the world! Also, we see this trend again in the New Testament between the Apostle Paul and Timothy where Paul says to his apprentice Timothy to hold on to the teachings that he has received from him which is preaching and teaching the gospel, in prayers and in the practice of spiritual disciplines 1 Timothy 4:6. Therefore, it is clear that anyone who wishes to be a teacher of the scriptures should endeavor to master the art of the trade that he/she seeks to become the master of. And by mastering I mean such a person should become what I like to call a reflective theologian. The latter is a term in personal development whereby a person learns to reflect on their actions in an attempt to learn from their experience. This view holds that when we as humans practice deep reflection on our past actions, it helps us in making better decisions as people in the future. And when this term is used in this seminary context, it simply means that a person becomes a better seminary student, minister, and teacher, when they are able to relate the present knowledge learned in formal educational context to their past or current experience. This is the whole focus of the book "Ghost of Seminary Past." It is meant to make seminarians and ministers or anybody thinking of teaching and leading another to faith to use as a tool to know how to do theology properly. The best thing about this book is that it is a practical tool that contains a lot of information and engages the readers to be a better Theological Reflective Practitioner even without having real-life ministerial experience which is a prerequisite for entering into seminary. Reason being that I have prayerfully shared my personal story, life, and heart for ministry which is gathered from my 18 years of ministry as a female minister both in a third world country as a Southern Christian from West Africa and from Ministering and being educated in Northern churches in the Western world. This gives me an added advantage to see and practice ministry from two different worlds therefore giving my readers an experience that they will not find easily in other theological books. Also, readers will find that in my application and use of the scripture I have applied unconventional methods of practice and synthesizing of my knowledge; this again is due to my experience and knowledge in other specialist fields such as health care, law, and business and personnel development skills that I have gathered over so many years in the educational system of Africa, Europe and in the United States. Hopefully, it is my desire and prayers that anyone who reads any of my books will continue to encounter the power of Christ Jesus who is the only PERFECT TEACHER. Therefore, I pray that as many that will engage in the reading of this text that they too will come to discover the many faces of images of God that is alive and breathing in the world today. Grace and Peace be upon all. Amen

2.1 SPIRITUAL AUTOBIOGRAPHY

2.1.1 My Story My Life

We know from the pastoral epistles of the Apostle Paul to the young Timothy what it takes to become a minister, what the apostle called "a good minister of Christ Jesus" (1 Tim. 4.6). This element of good is spoken several times in the Scriptures. Although the term "good" is relative, in this sense, I take it to mean the essential principles that every minister should have to master or develop the art of ministry. As described in the words of the St. Gregory the Great:

> "No one presumes to teach an art that he has not first mastered through study. How foolish it is therefore for the inexperienced to assume pastoral authority when the care of the souls is the art or arts...And yet, how often do they who are completely ignorant of spiritual precepts profess themselves, physicians of the heart, while anyone who is ignorant of the power of medicine is too embarrassed to be seen as a physician of the body."[1]

---

1 George E. Demacopoulos, *St Gregory the Great: the Book of Pastoral Rule* (St Vladimir Seminary Press: New York, 2007), 29-30.

It is in the light of this quotation that the inspiration for my Spiritual Autobiography is drawn. I have been serving as a minister for eighteen years in Nigeria, West Africa, and I have been serving as head executive leader in my local church; part of my role includes taking and making decisions that affect people's lives and the wellbeing of the local community. It is essential, therefore, that I master the act of ministry and keep my body, soul, and mind disciplined, so I can be attentive to what the Lord is saying about me and about my congregation.

My spiritual formation stems from my early childhood days. From a very young age, I was brought up in a family that believed in the importance of service, mission, vision, and selfless services to humanity. These are the values I have tried to live in my everyday life. I was born into a family of seven and with a sense of mission.

Both of my parents are clergy, and both are life members of the Bible Society of Nigeria. They are life members of the Christian Association of Nigeria and active in the Christian Council of Nigeria. My grandparents' Christian heritage comes from a combination of pioneers and founding elders of the Anglican church in the whole of the eastern region of Nigeria. They were some of the first knights of the Catholic movement in my country. They were known as the powerhouse and were one of those families that fought for independence during the time that Nigeria was under the rule of Great Britain.

My family background and Christian background became mixed as a result of both of my parents' childhoods: the doctrine of the Anglican faith and the tenets of the Catholic Faith became the basis of my faith. The Catholic Church played a greater role. It predominantly shaped my knowledge from age 3 to 5. Both parents eventually had a shift from Catholicism to Pentecostalism after a transformative move of the Holy Spirit in their lives. My mother became the first woman Pentecostal Minister in my country. This was at a time when women were not allowed to speak in public or hold any religious position. So, at a very young age, even before I was three, I was very much aware of ethical categories concerning faith, gender, power, status, tradition, belief, equality, and justice.

My experience with God began while in Sunday school classes where I was taught the essential principles of my faith, namely, how to love the Lord God wholeheartedly, true discipleship, being in tune with the Spirit of the Lord, and reaching out to a hurting world. In addition, at the age of seven, I was given an opportunity by my Sunday school teacher to form a children's dance group within the church and a children's choir called Baby Choir, which was made up of about 40 children, and guided by a Bible teacher from our Sunday school. This group became a social group for the children within my ministry, which attracted many young people in the community. We created our norms and expectations and our ages varied from age seven to around age sixteen. As we became older, we separated the group into two parts, called the Junior Choir and a new Baby Choir. I believe it was there that I developed my first leadership skill set.

My interest in theology began when I gave my first sermon at the age of ten. In 1997, I worked as a hospital administrator at a Christian hospital where I ministered to the sick patients, and this created a deeper desire in me to get involved more in the Church. After graduating with an associate degree in Health Education, I was given an opportunity to serve at the children's Ministry for Mothers and Babies. In 2003, I became involved in promoting and advocating against gun crimes, cultism, prostitution, corruption, and drug abuse in 5 different universities in the Southern part of the country. In 2007, I also advocated the right of the African Street child and care for underprivileged children in Edo State metropolis, thereafter, founding the first orphanage for street children in my local government, where I served and established a non-profit primary school to provide education for underprivileged children. All these different charitable activities deepened my desire to love and serve the Lord; they helped instill in me the passion for being a true disciple of Christ. This led me to begin to see God's essence in relationships and fellowship, and it created a quest of longing for God to use me as an instrument of peace in the world.

My journey did not end here. In 2008, after graduating and obtaining my master's degree in Human Resource Management with a concentration on Human development, I enrolled for non-certification classes at a local church in the city of Chester, England, United Kingdom. This led me to begin to see God's essence in relationships and fellowship. Thereafter, I applied for a self-study program in theology at the Bible College of Wales and was fortunate to have a mentor who is a theological scholar at the university. His guidance helped me shed more light on the subject. I realized that it was a very unique and interesting subject that not only enlightens one's mind but also helps to bring one more in tune with God and people. It helped me see God's relationship with everything he created; it opened my mind to realize that there is relativity with the divine in everything we see. It also came to my understanding that having a degree in divinity will help teach me more transferable skills and knowledge which are lacking in the society today, help me tackle basic societal issues such as human liberty, ethics, and the interplay between Church leadership, theology, psychology and culture.

Apart from the above events, one essential element that has highly sharped my spiritual formation is the influence, support, mentorship, and direction of my spiritual mother, who is also my biological mother, to whom I am grateful as her life and faith serve as a daily inspiration for me.

My mother taught me the essence of true disciples by her actions. At an early age, she prepared me for discipleship, teaching me various spiritual disciplines and practices, such as fasting on weekly and monthly bases, praying every fourth hour of the day (total of 9 times a day), serving the poor by caring for widows, orphans and the destitute, and keeping watch by having night vigils every first Tuesday of the month.

Worship was an essential part of my prayer time. Before any prayer is made we must worship to open up the doors of our hearts, spending daily time in reading the Bible, creating solitude—time alone just to be in God's presence—and the practice of life of celibacy. All these I have been practicing from childhood into my adult stage. This discipline has grown me in unimaginable ways, and it has opened my heart, mind, and body unto the Holy Spirit.

In addition, there have been other people that have been instrumental in my spiritual development over the years. For example, during my first year in seminary, I had the privilege of meeting a spiritual director, a minister in one of the faculties who served as my director for over three years. I decided to have a spiritual director who meets with me once every week, so I can keep watch and be accountable for my actions and inactions, helping me to keep to the spiritual disciplines I have acquired over the years. Also, I have been working as a volunteer with Hendrick Hospital as a chaplain for two years, where I visit and pray and sing to patients three times a week, sometimes more if the patient requests that they want me to pray with them. Four books have been instrumental in my spiritual growth during my seminary days; these are Eugene Peterson's *Christ Plays in Ten Thousand Places: A Conversation in Spiritual Theology*; Eugene Peterson's *Working the Angles*; and George E. Demacopoulos's *St. Gregory the Great: The Book of Pastoral Rule* and Jeffrey Greenman & George Kalantzis's *Life in the Spirit: Spiritual Formation in Theological Perspective*. Each author's view of pastoral care, ministry, and the proper function of a pastor in the Holy Church of Jesus has served as great tools for me. I will talk more about these books later on in the introduction chapter.

Drawing from above, my personal life experiences have greatly affected my identity and might have created some cultural biases, which are evident in my top five-leadership strengths according to Tom Rath & Barry Conchie's Strength Finder Test. The following was the result from the online test score that I took:

- Achiever
- Belief
- Learner
- Responsibility
- Self-Assurance

From the above list, my leadership strength as an Achiever helps me when learning to be goal-oriented; thus, whenever I set out for any task, I am very passionate about it and I can work for long hours. It does not matter how stressful it is, as long as I get the job done. I always achieve my set goals and aim for results. This has helped me to achieve a great deal and kept me focused. My bias here is a tendency of frustration and disappointment or breaking of relationships when my team is not doing well.

Secondly, my Belief leadership strength stems from coming from a family lineage of bishops, ministers, revolutionaries, politicians, and humanitarians from my grandparents, uncles, and parents. I have been brought up as a child to have and believe in certain core Christian values and come from a revolutionary family that believes in the concept of equal rights and justice. I believe that everything I have written thus far created this strong belief system in me, both in my spiritual and moral life as a humanitarian and an activist, having a sense of mission to God, then to the poor, which has influenced my campaigning for the plight of the poor within my community, founding of various charity organizations, campus fellowships, and football clubs and my life as a woman of God; whatever can impact lives has been my goal. Also, my leadership identity has the core strength of a learner, which has helped me to be open to new ideas, seek new ideas, be very innovative and accept change. I enjoy practicing new ideas and am always willing and ready to implement them. This strength helps me to think outside the box and has created a great drive in me for acquiring knowledge in various fields. My bias here will be the tendency to always want to change things, replace things, or try new things. There is the eagerness to constantly introduce change, and this may cause abrupt interruption of the system, create difficulty for the people or team to follow, and as is in all cases of change, there will be resistance and reaction, which if not properly monitored or resolved may affect the system so I have learned to be aware of this fact and try to walk with the Lord's timing. My identity is also shaped by my strength of Responsibility. This strength helps me to be committed, trusted, take responsibility for myself, be responsible for whatever is entrusted to my care, and be loyal and humble. This strength has helped me to be very reliable, to build a strong network and friendships within my workplace and community.

Lastly, my leadership strength Self-Assurance keeps me motivated at all times on any given task. I know what I want and know how to get it done; it is very easy for me to make a decision and take action, and I have the ability to seek information and answers from specialists and to take risks.

A leader's existence becomes dependent on the kind of power he/she possesses. Leaders use power to the extent that they control the immaterial and material within the environment.[2] The Bible supports this view where it states in the book of Luke 9:23-24, "Those who would be my disciples must deny themselves and take up their cross and follow me, for those who want to save their life will lose it but those who lose their life for me will save it."[3] The Bible also supported the denying of self in Matthew 20:28; there it reads, "Instead, whoever wants to become great among you must be your servant and whoever wants to be first must be your slave just as the Son of Man did not come to be served but to serve and to give his life as a ransom for many."[4] And as for the relinquishing

---

2   Lingenfelter, Sherwood G. *Leading Cross Cultural: Covenant Relationships for Effective Christian Leadership* (MI: Baker Academic, 2008), 49, 107-119.
3   Attridge, Harold W, *The Harper-Collins Study Bible* Eds. Wayne A. Meeks, et al.;(New York: HarperCollins, 1989), 1976.
4   Ibid., 1895.

of control, the Bible says in Luke 9:24, "Whoever loses their life for me will save it."[5] The above Biblical scriptures are in reference to the extent to which I exercise power within my ministry context in Africa.

In addition to the above, I took the personality and spiritual gifting text during my doctoral seminar and I learned more about how my spiritual gifts are related to my personality. For example, my spiritual gifts are Evangelism, faith, and Knowledge, while my personality DISC model test showed that in both "M" and " L" I am CS in two categories, which according to test result and my professor it is uncommon and unique, I was made to understand that it means that I was balanced. But the development side of it will mean that I have to be careful about taking too much on, so I don't burn out and I do agree this is true, because of my abilities and strength I tend to take on too much in serving and most times it affects my health. This is an area of development I am seeking healing from the Lord and trying to be aware of my weakness, as I continue to grow in my faith and walk with Christ.

In conclusion, I will like to end my personal spiritual autobiography by looking at the advice given by Apostle Paul to young Timothy. In 1Timothy 4:6, the Apostle Paul, who is the older mentor to Timothy, tells him to show himself to be a good minister of Christ, one that is nourished on the truth of the faith and of the good teaching that he has followed. From the strict literal interpretation of the context of the text, Paul advises Timothy to hold to the teaching he has received; this shows the importance of ministerial teaching.[6] Also in 1 Timothy 4:13 Paul says, "Until I come, devote yourself to the public reading of scripture, to preaching and to teaching." I consider these three points of Paul as essential to my formation; thus, as Paul rightly says, I work daily to equip

---

5   Ibid., 1976

6   Steven McKenzie and Stephen Haynes, *to each its own meaning: An Introduction to Each to Biblical criticisms* (Louisville: Westminster John Knox Press, 1999), 146-147.

myself for public reading by preparing a scriptural message. Devotion to prayer through reading of the psalms is one essential practice that I make sure I do. Prayer time with the Lord nine times daily, fasting, and the aforementioned practices have helped me to stay connected with God. Also, it has given me a sense of direction toward the ultimate plan of God in my life, to know His will and to do them in accordance with His word. These practices have helped me to keep watch over my soul, as Paul tells Timothy: "Watch your life and doctrine closely. Preserve them because if you do, you will save yourself and your hearers" (1 Tim. 4:16). Finally, I thrive on meditating on a set of scriptures day and night.[7] I do know that I am a fallible, weak creature in need of a savior, so I keep in mind that I can do all these through his grace alone, never seeing myself as obtaining perfection in this world, knowing that He alone is perfect and does his good works in and through me.

In addition, my spiritual formation has been influenced through the help of great pastoral literatures that I have been exposed to in the seminary. There are twenty-one books that have been formative to my spiritual growth over the many years of my seminary training around the world. These books are talked about extensively with references made to my ministry context in Africa. Seminarians, Ministers, and Laities will find that when doing ministry as ministers they are placed in a position of what I like to call a theological practitioner. In other words, when reading a theological work of art, a person is expected to do more than glazing over the work just for turning in a term paper or reading the book on the surface. In fact, a person is meant to immerse them-selves into the world of the author. Mary Clark Moshcella in her book *Ethnography as a Pastoral Practice: An Introduction*,[8] there she defines the metaphor Immersion to mean to be present and to participate in a

---

7   See also 1 Tim 2:5-6; Col. 4:17; 2 Tim 4:2; Titus 4:2; 1 Tim 3:16, 6:15-16; Titus 2:5,7; 3:4-7; Heb. 12:15; 2 John 1:18.

8   Mary clark Moschella, *ETHNOGRAPHY as a Pastoral Practice: An INTRODUCTION* (Ohio: The Pilgrim Press, 2008),168.

cultural setting that generates new knowledge. Same in engaging with any text and material the readers are expected to dive into the world of the author, by diving I mean when reading the material, readers are to read between the lines because every idea and comment of an author is an invitation to engage intellectually with the text and to dialog with the text subconsciously. By this, I mean that when reading a text there is an ongoing conversation between the reader and the text. Thus, applying this to the ministry setting, the readers should be able to see his/her ministerial context within the world of the author. Consequently, in reading theological text readers are expected to systematize every idea presented and generate new ideas as they conclude the reading. One of the methods that I have used over the years is to immerse my ministry context in the world of the text by asking How and What questions – My how questions are: How does this book fit in my context? How does this new idea compare to my own theology? and finally, how does this new idea /knowledge change my previous knowledge? And the "what questions" are - What are my expectations at the beginning of reading the text? What religious practices do I want to explore? What type of intellectual interpretation can I see in my own theology or my ministry context that needs change based on my new knowledge? And what is the rationale? What will be the scope of the intervention of my new knowledge (application) and finally what will be my limitation in applying the new knowledge? Once I have been able to answer these questions before, during, and after the reading then I have effectively immersed myself into the world of the text and I have given birth to a new self.

Bibliography

Benson, W Bruce. "Working the Angles: The Shape of Pastoral Integrity." *Word &World* 8, no. 1 (1988): 92-94. *ATLA Religion Database with ATLASerials*, EBSCO*host* (accessed March 11, 2016).

Collins, John J. *Introduction to the Hebrew Bible*. Minneapolis: Fortress Press, 2014.

Demacopoulos, George E., *St Gregory the Great: the Book of Pastoral Rule*.St Vladimir's Seminary Press: New York, 2007.

Jeffrey, Greenman, & George Kalantzis. *Life in the Spirit: Spiritual Formation in Theological Perspective*. Illinois: IVP Academic, 2010.

Lischer, Richard. "The Word That Moves: The Preaching of Martin Luther King, Jr." Review of Theology Today 46 (July 1989): 169-182

Luibheid, Colm. *John Cassian Conferences: Translation and Preface*. Paulist Press: New York, 1985.

McKenzie, Steven, Stephen Haynes, *To Each Its own meaning: An Introduction to Biblical Criticisms and Their Application*. Louisville: Westminster John Knox Press, 1999.

Moschella, Mary Clark. *ETHNOGRAPHY as a Pastoral Practice: An INTRODUCTION*. Ohio: The Pilgrim Press, 2008.

Schwanda, Tom. "Christ plays in ten thousand places: a conversation in spiritual theology." *Christian Education Journal* 4, no. 2 (September 2007): 444-447. *ATLA Religion Database with ATLASerials*, EBSCO*host* (accessed March 11, 2016).

Stewart, John W. "Working the Angles: The Shape of Pastoral Integrity." *Reformed Journal* 39, no. 5 (May 1989): 24-26. *ATLA Religion Database with ATLASerials*, EBSCO*host* (accessed March 11, 2016).

Time Sensing, *"African America*n Preaching *" Homiletical Sensing, 11 March* 2016, http://blogs.acu.edu/sensingt/resources/

Time Sensing, *"African America*n Preaching *" Homiletical Sensing, 12 March* 2016, http://blogs.acu.edu/sensingt/resources/

Willard, Dallas, The spirit of the disciple. (New York: HarperCollins, 1990), chap.1, (accessed August 11, 2016).

Tozer, A.W. The Pursuit of God (Michigan: Baker Publishing Group, 2013), chap. 1, (accessed August 14, 2016).

3.1 INTRODUCTION

3.1.1 SPIRITUAL FORMATION

3.1.2 The Heart of a Disciple

The desire of becoming a disciple of Christ in our contemporary culture is very challenging. There are many in the church of God who are tempted to be seen as being spiritually formed and equipped, and some place themselves as spiritual directors having authoritative voices in the holy church, aspiring only to have glory and honor. In their deepest heart, they know that they are unworthy to be a disciple of Christ whose duty is to minister to the church and the world around them. Such persons have gotten into the habit of practicing virtues solely by the means of vanity of the heart.[9] Being a Christian that is "Christ-like" is a serious business and walking the path of discipleship is "a long journey." Thus, when Christ gave the invitation by saying, Come and follow me, what he meant was, come and suffer with me. Come and drink of my cup and take my yoke upon you. Such a call is made to the whole person (body, soul, and mind). As Proverbs 1:21 simply states, lady wisdom shouts in the street, she lifts her voice in the square calling. This invitation is opened to all people, open to the souls whose hearts hear wisdom's voice

---

9   George E. Demacopoulos, *St Gregory the Great: the Book of Pastoral Rule* (Vladimir Seminary Press: New York, 2007), 29-30.

and submit to her instructions. Thus, when the soul becomes receptive to this voice and it begins to gaze solely on the radiance of the presence of its object (God), it is at that point that the whole person is put under subjection, under the power of the Holy Spirit. Again, it is important to state that no one should ever think to themselves that it is by their own effort and strength that they have obtained spiritual gifts, but all should know that this is a divine call that comes from the Holy Spirit who becomes the center point of the soul.

Also, this call is a call to join in the Holy Trinitarian relationship with the divine, which is brought about through the grace of the Holy Spirit by an act of faith. Tozer calls this kind of faith "faith in operation" (cf. John 3:15; 7:16). He writes that this kind of faith takes place when the soul gazes upon the saving God, an outward-looking kind of faith, where the object of the gaze is God Himself.[10] This is what it means to be spiritually formed or to be engaged in spiritual disciplines. Spiritual formation is the end product of spiritual disciplines; it is about innovation of the whole person, and it is the becoming of something new. It is not to be taken as something that takes place immediately; rather, it requires a consistent effort and investment over time (2 Cor 5:17, Gal 4:19, Rom 8:29 and Rom 12:2).[11] For example, the historical Jesus was seen throughout the course of history practicing spiritual disciplines such as worship, prayer, fellowship, evangelism, fasting, service, reading scriptures, teaching, contemplation, discernment, resting, communion, celebration, and others.

In addition, Philip Sheldrake defines spiritual practices as practices that bring the whole body under the submission of the Holy Spirit. For him, these disciplines can take the form of *ascetical/monastic practices*

---

10   A.W. Tozer, The Pursuit of God (Michigan: Baker Publishing Group, 2013), chap. 7, (accessed August 14, 2016).

11   Houston Heflin, "Spiritual Formation," Class Lecture, Spiritual Formation from Abilene Christian University, Abilene, TX, August 8, 2016.

such as abstinence from worldly pleasures, *mystical practices* such as contemplation, *activities practices* such as glorifying God through the work that we do, and *prophetic critical practices* such as extreme commitment to social justice.[12]

Also, Dallas Willard in his book, *Spirits of the Disciplines*, speaks about spiritual disciplines as something that should be taken as meaningless or useless by themselves; they are useful practices only when they work within us to bring us closer to God. For Willard, spiritual discipline brings about the fulfillment of the whole person and the deliverance of the body from the powers of sin. The whole purpose of life is for an individual to be reunited with God through his son.[13] In addition, Tozer concludes that the sole purpose of creation is for humans to know God and his son Jesus Christ whom God has sent. This he calls eternal life.[14] Therefore, eternal life does not begin after death, but we experience it here on earth. Eternal life is the point whereby God touches the believer with his redeeming power and draws the Christian believer into a life of interaction with Himself and creation.[15] This means God is present here on earth and can only be found by those who diligently seek him; the whole economy of salvation is for God to bring us into a right relationship with him, bringing back the original creator-creature relationship that God shared with humans at the Garden of Eden.

---

12 Philip Sheldrake, Spirituality: A Brief History. (Chichester: John Wiley & Sons, 2013), 15-17.

13 Dallas Willard, *The Spirit of the Disciple*. (New York: HarperCollins, 1990), chap.1, (accessed August 11, 2016).

14 Tozer, Chap.1, accessed August 11, 2016.

15 Greenman, Jeffrey & George Kalantzis. Life in the Spirit: Spiritual Formation in Theological Perspective. (Illinois: IVP Academic, 2010), 50-51.

4.1 SPIRITUAL FORMATION REFLECTIONS

The great Apostle Paul in his epistle to his beloved Timothy was to hold to what the Apostle calls the essential spiritual principles that make a good minister. In this chapter, I am going to look at the work of several Christian spiritual formation Gurus of contemporary times whose work has been very instrumental in my faith work in becoming a minister of the gospel. This chapter will examine in an extensive discourse addressing the question - what are the good practices that can help a disciple to achieve these principles? In answering this question, I have selected four books that share light on the subject matter, which I have used as a formative tool in ministerial life. I have chosen four books: Eugene H. Peterson's *Christ Plays in Ten thousand Places: A Conversation in Spiritual Theology*; Peterson's *Working the Angles*, George E. Demacopoulos's *St Gregory the Great: the Book of Pastoral Rule* and Jeffrey Greenman & George Kalantzis's *Life in the Spirit: Spiritual Formation in Theological Perspective*. I will be looking at each author's view of spiritual formation and the responsibility of a discipleship in the Holy Church of Jesus. Finally, I will offer my personal perspective of these two aspects on the training and spiritual disciplines that helps a Christian to be spiritually formed.

4.1.1 Peterson, Eugene H. Christ Plays in Ten thousand Places: A Conversation in Spiritual Theology.

Peterson takes Spirituality to a whole different level with his book, "allowing the Lord to play in us." He draws his inspiration from the Gerard Manley Hopkins poem. Peterson sees spiritual growth in believers not as a product of personal achievement; rather, spiritual growth comes through a selfless submission to the divine presence. Schwanda was of the view that Peterson preferred to use the term spiritual theology because the primary focus of his book is to recover the spirituality that has been lost in modern believers.[16] When a believer give a total submission of themselves, i.e. the body, soul and their mind, to God, this helps to open their minds to be more receptive to the wonders of God in creation. God's essence begins to renew the mind, thereby lifting up the mind to a contemplative state where it begins to see itself and creation (community) in relativity with the Divine plan. All of this has a Trinitarian relationship—each one depending on the other to fulfill God's greatest plan for humankind.[17] This Trinitarian relationship reveals Christ's plan both in creation, in the history of salvation and community.

According to Peterson, this plan calls for an active involvement of a Christian belief in a participative life of faith. For example, he talks about the believer's deliberate withdrawal from the business of everyday life to develop a spiritual mindset whereby they take sabbatical time off

---

16 Schwanda, Tom. 2007. "Christ plays in ten thousand places: a conversation in spiritual theology." *Christian Education Journal* 4, no. 2: 444-447. *ATLA Religion Database with ATLASerials*, EBSCO*host* (accessed August 11, 2016).

17 Colm Luibheid, *John Casssian Conferences: Translation and Pre*face (Paulist Press: New York, 1985), 102-103. "Therefore, if we wish our prayers to reach upward to the heaven and beyond we must ensure that our mind is cleared of every earthly defect and cleansed of all passion's grip and is so light of itself that its prayer, free of sin's weighty load, will rise upward to God.

to rest, so they can spend time in contemplation about God and the things he has created. When this discipline is done properly, the resultant effect is that the Christians become aware that they are not called to be spectators in the world but they are called to be in active partnership with the divine in carrying out the plan. Therefore, humans are co-creators whose purposes are not only to create on earth[18] but also to care for the things which God has created and called into existence.

4.1.2 Peterson's Working the Angles: The Shape of Pastoral Integrity

In Stewart John's summary review of Peterson's work *Working the Angles: The Shape of Pastoral Integrity*. He noted that Peterson holds the view that contemporary disciple's true discipline should be seen in the manner in which he works his angles.[19] He listed a few spiritual disciplines that he considers to be essential for the development of true discipleship: developing an honest heart for prayer, Bible study, and spiritual direction. Developing a spiritual mindset by taking weekly Sabbatical time off to be with God, spending time in contemplation about God and the things he has created are also important. Peterson warns that all these require the training of the mind to become conscious of what God is doing in the whole human person and in creation. Peterson gives a provocative view on how each angle can best be shaped; for him the art of prayer and reading the Scripture should be an essential daily discipline for every minister.[20]

---

18 John J. Collins. *Introduction to the Hebrew Bible* (Minneapolis: Fortress Press, 2014), 80-82.

19 Stewart, John W. 1989. "Working the Angles: The Shape of Pastoral Integrity." Reformed *Journal* 39, no. 5: 24-26. *ATLA Religion Database with ATLASerials*, EBSCO*host* (accessed August 11, 2016).

20 Bruce W. Benson, "Working the Angles: The Shape of Pastoral Integrity." *Word & World* 8, no. 1 (1988): 92-94. *ATLA Religion Database with ATLASerials*, EBSCO*host* (accessed January 11, 2016).

To Peterson, too many American mainline churches have abandoned their calling by not teaching their members how to work the essential discipline that is needed to be formed spiritually as a disciple of Christ. In *Working the Angles*, Peterson gives a provocative view on how each angle can best be sharpened. For him, the art of prayer should be an essential daily discipline. He urges believers to develop an art of prayer that involves praying the book. This to him was an essential part of spiritual formation. Prayer should be accompanied by learning prayer language. He invites us to embrace the reading of Psalms. For him, while most of the scripture speaks to us, the language of Psalms prays for us. They help us hear what God is saying to us out of his word in the Scripture. Benson sees the life of prayer as our antiphonal response to the music of God, always there for those who have ears to hear.[21]

In addition, Peterson's second "angle" is reading the scripture. He emphasizes the importance of contemplative exegesis on the word, by which he means the capacity of a believer to listen openly and submissively to God's decision, which will help to sharpen him. God uses the Scriptures as a means of revealing himself to us. He noted that contemporary mainline churches have lost the exegetical technique of seeing the scripture as the living word of God, which is still effective in this modern world. He accused mainline Christians of regarding the Bible as lifeless and having nothing to do with the world we live in today. For him, everything in the world of culture can be made sense of without putting God in the equation, but we can never make sense of the Scripture without God. And as Tozer puts it, God can never be known in pieces; God hides Himself so that he can be sought after, for only the mighty longing souls find Him.[22]

---

21 Benson, W. Bruce. 1988. "Working the Angles: The Shape of Pastoral Integrity." *Word & World* 8, no. 1: 92-94. *ATLA Religion Database with ATLASerials*, EBSCO*host* (accessed August 11, 2016), 86.
22 Tozer, Chap.1, accessed August 11, 2016.

In addition, Richard Lischer supports this view in his review of the traditional understanding of King's background in his article "The Word That Moves: The Preaching of Martin Luther King, Jr." According to Lischer, the Black preacher gets his authority from the pulpit. The words in the Scripture are not functioning as a theoretical base for action; rather, the Scriptural words are a kind of action that cannot legitimately be separated from the struggles, temptations, sufferings, and hopes of the people. Following this view in this context, the believer gets his strength from a continual practice of the daily reading of the scripture.[23] Tim Sensing in his powerful Homiletics view of African American Preaching quotes Peterson's view on how oral utterances connect to narrative discourses to produce a Bakhtin's dialogic framework. This method creates a synergy of many voices. The reader begins to share in the story of the narrative, thereby making the stories in the narrative a part of his life. For Sensing, there are two messages at the same time, namely a message of acceptance from the words, which are written, and a message of liberation. This is what Peterson means when he says the Psalms prays for us, when the believers read aloud the Psalms during prayers; he or she begins to interact with the text. Two voices are brought under supplication before God: one is the sound of the believer's voice and the other is the voice of the psalm. The content and meaning of the words that are spoken becomes the petition of the minister; the minister's use of the words in her prayers becomes her acceptance, which at the end of the prayers he becomes liberated from whatever burden he has taken unto the Christ.[24]

The final "angle" that Peterson talked about is the need for renewal of the practice of spiritual direction. Spiritual direction is an honest dialog that takes place when two people agree to give their full attention to

---

23 Richard Lischer, "The Word That Moves: The Preaching of Martin Luther King, Jr." Review of Theology Today 46 (July 1989): 169-182.

24 Tim Sensing, *"African American* Preaching" *Homiletical Sensing, 11 March* 2016, http://blogs.acu.edu/sensingt/resources/

what God is doing in one or both of their lives. He sees this as the place where the development of faith begins, and a time when the believers learn to trust God, to walk under the guidance of another to whom he becomes accountable for his actions. As such, the director helps him keep watch over his soul.

4.1.3 George E. Demacopoulos, St Gregory the Great: the Book of Pastoral Rule

Demacopoulos introduces St Gregory the Great's work on pastoral rule in five-part essays. Each essay is exquisitely crafted into several heading that seem closely connected in some part with Peterson's book, *Working the Angles*. Part of Demacopoulos' book speaks extensively about the qualification of anyone who comes to the position of spiritual director. To Demacopoulos, the role of a minister within the church is one that has to do with what he called spiritual leadership. A spiritual director to him is saddled with the sole responsibility of taking care of the souls. He sees the minister's role as not to be taken lightly but one that requires strict discipline in the Scriptures, which he feels can only be gotten from seminary theological training. Studying the word has to be a part of the minister and the minister should be seen living it out. In part three, Demacopoulos talks about Spiritual Director. He gives the illustration of David and Prophet Nathan reproving the king's sin. St Gregory's view of a spiritual director is like that; it is an act that should be done in the spirit of love and understanding, knowing that we are sinners and less than perfect. The mind should always be kept clean of guilt; as such, a spiritual director needs to be a person who can hold the directee accountable for his actions.

4.1.4 Greenman, Jeffrey & George Kalantzis. Life in the Spirit: Spiritual Formation in Theological Perspective.

Greenman and Kalantzis in their thirteen-part essay have a clear-cut definition of what spiritual formation is and the importance of being formed spiritually. Spiritual formation is man's continuing response to the reality of God's grace. It is the process of reshaping and redeveloping the inner self of the Soul until it has to a great degree the inner nature of Christ.[25] It is the work of the Holy Spirit, and it is lived out in the community of faith. Greenman and Kalantize list the following characteristics as being important in spiritual formation: it is a gradual and progressive movement and spiritual growth of the whole person; its primary aim is cultivating and developing an intimate relationship with God; it is dynamic in nature in that it focuses on the continued response to the reality of God; it is wholly God initiated and its transformation is brought about by God's saving grace; it is the recognition of the saving power of grace and fallible nature of man; it involves a grace-bound discipline of forgiveness, reconciliation and confession and it requires intentional actions of faith. Green and Kalantize see the continual, habitual practices of spiritual discipline as reading Christ into the Heart of the saint. For them, a close look at the lives of the historical saints will help contemporary believers understand what spiritual disciplines are and in pursuing them. Some of the specific disciplines listed are the practice of *Lectio Divina* prayer (which is reading the scriptures with an intention of deep transformation of one's soul by an intentional act of living out the text), a meditation on the scripture by the recital of the scripture out loud, creating time for centered prayer which is a higher level of contemplation and the practice of spiritual direction.

---

25 Greenman, Jeffrey & George Kalantzis. Life in the Spirit: Spiritual Formation in Theological Perspective (Illinois: IVP Academic, 2010), 24, 25, 46.

In conclusion, the question is: what are the essential important spiritual practices that make a good disciple? And what are some of the good practices that can help develop and grow disciples? To answer this question, I will like to look at the canonical interpretation of the term "good disciple." In 1Timothy 4:6, the Apostle Paul tells Timothy, "Show yourself to be a good minister (disciple) of Christ that is nourished on the truth of the faith and of the good teaching that you have followed." From the strict literal interpretation of the context of the text, Paul advises Timothy to adhere to the teaching he has received. This includes ceaseless prayer life, solitary time with God, fasting to subject the flesh to stress, service to the poor, and sacrament and communal living. These were all practices and teachings of the disciples that Jesus taught them.[26] Thus it is only when a believer's soul becomes submitted to the power of the Holy Spirit that he/she can be truly formed, that such a soul has been redeemed, that such a soul has received the greatest of creation, which is to know God and His only Son Jesus Christ whom he sent.

Bibliography

Bruce, Benson W. "Working the Angles: The Shape of Pastoral Integrity." *Word & World* 8, no. 1 (1988): 92-94. *ATLA Religion Database with ATLASerials*, EBSCO*host* (accessed March 11, 2016).

Demacopoulos, George E., *St Gregory the Great: the Book of Pastoral Rule.*St Vladimir's Seminary Press: New York, 2007.

Harold, Attridge W. *The Harper-Collins Study Bible* Eds. New York: HarperCollins, 1989

Luibheid, Colm. *John Cassian Conferences: Translation and Preface.* Paulist Press: New York, 1985.

---

26 Steven McKenzie, Stephen Haynes, To each its own meaning: An Introduction to Each to Biblical criticisms (Louisville: Westminster John Knox Press, 1999), 146-147.

McKenzie, Steven, and Stephen Haynes. *To each its own meaning: An Introduction to Each to Biblical criticism.* Louisville: Westminster John Knox Press, 1999.

Schwanda, Tom. "Christ plays in ten thousand places: a conversation in spiritual theology." *Christian Education Journal* 4, no. 2 (September 2007): 444-447. *ATLA Religion Database with ATLASerials,* EBSCO*host* (accessed January 11, 2016).

Sherwood, Lingenfelter G. *Leading Cross-Cultural: Covenant Relationships for Effective Christian Leadership.* MI: Baker Academic, 2008.

Stewart, John W. "Working the Angles: The Shape of Pastoral Integrity." *Reformed Journal* 39, no. 5 (May 1989): 24-26. *ATLA Religion Database with ATLASerials,* EBSCO*host* (accessed January 11, 2016).

5.1 BOOK REVIEW READING TOOL

In each book review, readers will find that my theological interpretation was extensively from my African Homiletical lens which is colored with an ecumenical centric worldview which comes from my exposure from worshiping, fellowshipping, praying, studying, and celebrating with women and men from different denominations and walks of life. Thus, it is important that when reading each review that the readers try to fit in his/her own world into the world by this I mean one's ministerial context so as to fully appreciate the message of the author by intentionally becoming a theological practitioner. The latter term in my view is used to describe a faith seeker who is open to new ideas without any feeling of judgment he/ she approaches the book as a learner whose mindset intends to engage the creative piece of writing art with an attitude of making and appreciating inquiring into the claims that are made irrespective of truthful calls that he/she has made. Rather a good learner comes to a piece of creative informative art by application. For it is in the application that one comes to discover the rightness or the wrongness of anyone because, in every ministerial context, Ministers, clergies, laity, students of theology, and members are engaging and dealing with living human documents of complex beings which we call people. Therefore, it is my hope that at the end of each book reading that the reader should attempt to engage the questions giving by providing honest answers to how they think they can apply the new knowledge in their faith walk.

5.1.1. Christ and Culture, H. Richard Niebuhr, Harper Collins, New York, 1996.

Rev. Awele Ilobah, Dish (Ed), LLB (Law), MA. (HRM), MA. (DIV) Doctorate Candidate, Hadin Simmons Theological Seminary, San Antonio, Texas.

Review Year

Spring, 2018, Dmin.

Authors Intention

His aim is to help theological students and bible teachers on how to help their community of faith do theology properly in the face of changing circumstances in the world that threatens their faith.

Keywords

God-Historical Jesus – Church -Culture-scientific – Faith – Bible - Transformer

Thesis Claim

Richard Niebuhr claims that as human we are made in the image of God and therefore we share a certain attribute with God such as the ability to create, thus he sees man as a possessor of freewill then he sees humans as obedient citizen both to divine law and to natural law and lastly, he sees humans as a responder.

Introduction

Over the years philosophers and theologians have struggled to understand how best to determine and synthesize the amalgamation of various differences and similarities that co-exist between the material world (scientific) and the non-material world (faith/ religion). One of the first philosophers that drew attention to this tension that exists was no other person than the great Philosopher Tertullian, in this famous word.

"What has Jerusalem to do with Athens, the Church with the Academy and the Christian with the heretic? After Jesus we have no need of speculation, after the Gospel no need of research."—Tertullian[27] Here, Tertullian emphasizes the divide that exists between these two worlds and the tension it has created for Christians. It is no surprise that after many centuries both philosophers and theologians have come to rustle with these same issues but none has come close to the work of H. Richard Niebuhr (1894-1962), professor of ethics at Yale Divinity School-gave a brilliant rational and philosophical ethical examination of the tension that exists between both worlds, and not only that, he came up with five paradox synthesizing ways that believers use to rationalize and deal with the issue of Christ and Culture. Thus, in his classic book *"Christ and Culture"* Niebuhr sets out to uncover the problems that have to do with the relationship between a faith community and its surroundings, thus *his aim is to help theological students and bible teachers on how to help their community of faith do theology properly in the face of changing circumstances in the world that threatens their faith.* This he does by helping them to understand that there exist various ways people interpret and practice their faith differently depending on what paradox they are working from. (xvi-xix) Thus, Niebuhr's intention is to provide believers of his time with what he considered practical tools that are useful for the amalgamating and synthesizing methods of Christ and culture that are for resolving some of the issues faced by the church in the society today. In fact, this writer believes that Niebuhr's work is still much useful for today's 21st-century Christians. Consequently, his thesis holds that as human, we are made in the image of God and therefore we share a certain attribute with God such as the ability to create, thus he sees man as a creator (possessor of free will) then he sees humans as obedient citizen (both to divine law and to natural law) and lastly, he sees humans as a responder. (able to adapt to change) Thus, for him

---

27 https://www.adamsetser.com/blog/2015/10/20/
    what-has-jerusalem-to-do-with-athens

human knowledge comes from the community, and that humans come to know things based on their individual experiences in life, as lived in their various communities. Secondly, he claimed that because no two human experiences are the same, there exists a multiplicity of meaning surrounding interpretations, mostly with biblical interpretations; therefore, there cannot be any single /universal Christian ethical principle that should be placed above the others because every believer sees the world from different mental constructs and share different worldviews. Lastly, Niebuhr claims that the Christian life moves between the poles of God in Christ as known through faith and the Bible, and God in nature as known through reason in culture. (Xlii)

Furthermore, to best explain what this means, Niebuhr listed five cardinal points from which different believers see/interpret the scripture in relation to the world around them. These are as follows: *Christ of Culture, Christ and Culture, Christ against Culture, Christ above Culture, and Christ the Transformer of Culture.* Here, Niebuhr begins his explanation from the point that the majority of Christians fall under the *Christ against Culture model;* there exists the conception that because Jesus is the new law, all laws from the community are false. Also, there are general notions that as Christians our morality should be drawn from the person of Christ and no other way. As such anything outside of this comes short of authentic Christianity. (Xliv) But, Niebuhr sees this view as a narrow view and unhealthy way of doing theology. For him, historical Jesus did not come to abolish the law, nor did he change the culture of the people, but that because Jesus teachings threatened the culture of the people that was why he was rejected and the more reason they threatened to kill him. Although Niebuhr disputes the fact that the Christian faith is one faith that demands total submission to the lordship of Christ, and it is a faith that draws man's hope to another world which is unseen thereby depriving man in the insecure social world, he suggests that this is not the right way of doing theology, rather the Christian should be relational to God and to all that He has created. (9-20) Thus, for him, Jesus lived on earth as a son to the father but in relationship to the world. Jesus being God and becoming a man means that Jesus lived in Culture. In addition, Niebuhr defined culture as anything that has to do with the languages, habits, ideals, beliefs, customs, inherited artifacts, science, art, inventions, technology, etc. (32-33) Interestingly, Niebuhr believes that culture has to do with what is good for everyone in the community. In other words, every society considers itself the architect or source (center) of value from which meaning comes. (36) Obviously, this point drives home for this writer as she has always found herself and her congregation struggling with how best to inculcate the Christian gospel into the cultural life of the people. One of the ways her African Pentecostal congregation has done this is the incorporation of the playing of drums, clapping of hands during worship, and dancing during worship for her community as Africans this is their identity and the way her community interprets the gospel. This writer believes this is what Niebuhr is talking about when he says meaning comes from the community. (Africans hold a belief that life as we know it is made up of spiritual and physical world thus to be an African Christian means to live between the physical world and spiritual world). Consequently, this model describes a set of believes that holds strong negative view against culture. This set of people sees themselves as a third race apart from Jews, and Gentiles, in fact, they see themselves as different and peculiar citizens of the world. They don't see any good in the world; they go with the Tertullian's view of "what does Jerusalem has to do with Athens" they are strongly against science. In the contemporary time, this may be believers who do not believe in war or abortion or may refuse the use of any medical drugs because of their faith. Another name for this group is called exclusive Christianity.

Although Niebuhr rejects this form of faith practice as radical, he still acknowledges that the Christian faith demands a radical separation from material things.

Again, this writer believes that Niebuhr's view was right, but it lacks some precision and practical ways on how to synthesize. In her practice as a minister, these writers believe that the church should not separate itself from the world, because it does not operate in a vacuum rather the church is a part of a community and it interacts with a community. In fact, she believes that ministry cannot be done in isolation. But the proper way should be having a yardstick within which to determine what the correct ethical principle should be and this should be done on a case-to-case basis. For example, in the Africa context, there is the practice of paganism and animism, but once a believer gets converted he/she is asked to surrender their idols for destruction and give a complete devotion to Yahweh God. This is a complete isolation against the traditional gods in the culture because her community does not associate and part-takes in pagan festivals or worships. Again, in the same context, there exists the practice of polygamy which is a traditionally acceptable custom of the land, such as it was in ancient near eastern culture, thus this means that majority of the congregations are first-generation Christians meaning in their families they have no Christian heritage. Thus, almost every family comes from a polygamous home. The way her church has dwelt with this issue unlike other mother churches in her community dwelt with it at a time when Christianity was gaining grounds these churches asked their men to choose one of the wife and ask the other wife and her children to leave the home and disassociate himself from them. This brought destruction of homes and resistance to the faith. But for this writer's ministry, they allowed these families to come to Christ and ask them to choose a wife or abandon their children, but her church doesn't allow these man or their wives to hold any eldership or deacon position, their families are allowed to stay together, but their children are thought the essential principle of the Christian faith and are not allowed to marry more than one wife. This is her ministry's belief that as children become the second generation of Christians this will eventually change the traditional custom of the land, but the most essential thing for her ministry is applying love and peace so that families can be in union with each other and with God. So, the church allows them to meet the Lord or come to God from whatever position or stage they are in their life.

Thus, this writer believes that this what Niebuhr is talking about when he says there should be integration of the two worlds. (69)

Next, Niebuhr talks about this second paradox, which he called the *Christ of Culture model.* This set of people sees Christ as the heroes of the society, the fulfillment of their hope and aspiration and holiest spirit. They understand Christ through culture. For them, the work of Christ is the training of men and women in the social world to be better men and women in the next world to come. They see the Christian faith as a religion rather than as a new society. Niebuhr sees this group as having less resistance to their faith rather people will have resistance only towards doctrinal teachings and practices. But, he does not believe that this kind of mental construct provides a better solution to the tension. For instance, A modern-day believer may ask the question: What does it mean for the 21s-century American Christian to pray to a God of ancient first-century Christian? Niebuhr believes that there is no resemblance between the two cultures and as such contemporary Christians will have to find a way to deal with the tension. Here, he talks about how modern believers try to reproduce the culture in which Jesus lived, but because of the gap that exists between both worlds, it is impossible because of the differences in culture and the time period. Rather, a better way should be to learn how to synthesis the meaning between both worlds by brings both worlds together. Based on this, this writer will like to add that a good example of how Christians can bridge this gap is by designing a good biblical sermon. This will be a sermon that will draw from the myths, languages, symbols, and metaphors of the local congregation used in a preaching service or bible study time so that the people can relate to what the verse is saying, and the message comes alive to the community. For instance, in Africa during this writer's biblical exegesis she does not only try to move between the English language and the ten different local languages, but she has to look for local words in her delivering of her sermon that can capture the true meaning of the verse, and sometimes there are no words her dialect for the English word, where this is the case, she has to resort to developing new meaning from the experiences of her congregation and she allows the Holy Spirit to lead her inspiration so that people can receive that word that the Lord has for the community. This writer believes that this is what Niebuhr means when he says that the community gives new meaning, or it is through meaning that knowledge comes.

Also, another example of this in the writer's context is the fact that her ministry is seen as a ministry founded by a woman and as such has so many back clashes and resistance from the traditional rulers, because in her Africa traditional society and the practice of the ancient Benin land there is a belief that as a woman you cannot hold property, speak in public, and you cannot be educated, you are required to follow the lead of a man and should never preside over a man. Obviously, since the act of ministry involves presiding and instructing over men and women alike, there is a tension against her being a woman but not against the word of God that she preaches. In addition, another good example from her African context is the rise of African Christianity and African theology which is now taking shape in the world today, it is true that the African society is now witnessing a huge rise as never before seen due to the ability and recognition by contemporary Africa Pentecostal churches who are now able to inculcate the Christian gospel into the African way of life, so religion as we now come to it has become an authentically an African thing. In fact, the Africans no longer see the Christian gospel as being foreign, but they see it as an authentically African religion or faith. Thus, the God of the patriarchs is no longer the God of the old, but it is seen as the God of the new, and he is referred to as the God of the African people. (109)

Next is the *Christ above culture paradox*, this set of people holds the view that there exists a divine imperative and there exists a genuine discontinuity between both worlds, in fact, they hold that the natural less- values and imperative is not the same as the divine values and imperative. Another name of this set is called the church of the center they believe that nature is founded by God and Jesus is a ruler of the world, some members of this group can be radical, and some may have a center belief, and others may recognize the primacy of grace. They believe that Christians should only live according to the rules and laws of Jesus Christ. But, Niebuhr does not agree with this stand, he believes that to live in accordance with the rule of Christ is to live in accordance with the rule of nature. This to Niebuhr is what makes a believer a good Christian. For him, a person is said to be a good Christian if he/she abides by certain social standards. (121) In other words, a person that pays his tax, gives to charity, treats his neighbor well, abide by state laws is called a good Christian. Here, there is a convergence of two kingdoms -the kingdom of the world and the kingdom of Christ. For this reason, Niebuhr believes that all culture is relative to God as such God is the ruler and creator of the heavenly world and He is still the ruler and creator of the physical world. (131) Again, this writer agrees with this point, for her, this point drives home to the African epistemological believes of the existence of life. For Africans life is made of two worlds, the physical world, which we see, and the spiritual world, which is immaterial, and both worlds co-exist. This is seen practice by both the African Pentecostal and Evangelicals Christians alike. Thus, within the African religion there exists the belief of the existence of demonic accessorial spirits and evil spirits that are operating and hindering the modern believers. African evangelical ministries and even the traditional churches like the Catholic Church cannot exist if they fail to recognize the operation of these African believers because this is within the worldview of African people. For to be an African means to live within two worlds, this writer believes that this is a proper way of synthesizing this principle of the Christ above culture model.

In addition, Niebuhr talks about the *Christ and Culture paradox model*. This group is describing as a dualist group. They are neither left nor right group. They see their loyalty to Christ as being responsible to the world. They are not radical in the thinking neither are they standing at the center. Rather, they see the difference between what it means to be loyal to God and where to draw the line of being responsible to culture. Most importantly, they recognize that humans are fallen creatures in need of grace and they also believe that grace comes through the redemptive work of Christ and that it is made available to all humans. A good example of this is the theology of Apostle Paul. The later saw Jesus as the judgment of culture and also as the redeemer of Culture. Hence, this set of people believes that culture and Christ must be affirming as having importance. In other words, they must live in peaceful co-existence with one another. Although this writer agrees with some of the points that Niebuhr makes in this paragraph but she wonders what Niebuhr view will be in extreme cases where there is a cultural change demanding the change of faith let's say a Muslim government comes into power and demands all Christians to convert to Islam or where a traditional pagan ruler declares a pagan god as the god of the people as it is happening now presently in this writer's context, she wonders what Niebuhr will say of her congregation and millions of Christians who have refused to join the monarch, although some churches and denominations have accepted to partake in traditional gods worship but her and her congregation took a stand not to join in and are now being persecuted and the majority of people are being killed and removed from homes and jobs. Because of this, this writer believes that there can never be an absolute joining between culture and Christ because to do so is to place Christ in the same position with the world and to disregard the divinity of the Divine. As Niebuhr himself agrees that there is an absolute with the divine and if this is the case there must be an absolute where the culture has to stop, and Christ has to be chosen and elevated above culture. Although, Niebuhr links this to the greatest commandment principle of loving thy neighbor as meaning being in a relationship with him/her, but he pointed out that sometimes we have to take a stand to place restrictions on our neighbors if they are to do us harm. (186)

Lastly, Niebuhr talks about *Christ as the transformer of the church paradox model* this set of people holds the natural world as being corrupt and they believe that God tries the mind and holds the sub-consciousness. This group believes that all culture lies under the judgment of God. They see culture as self-destructive. But they believe that Christians must carry out cultural work in obedience to the lord. Also, they are more interested in what will be given at the end and about the redemption of the world. (195) A good proponent of this thought is St Augustine who believed that certain people were elected to be saved and that these people were different from others. (216) Again, Niebuhr is not in favor of this kind of thinking. He sees it as being too narrow-minded and radical. For him, it is important for believers to realize that no one shares an absolute knowledge about the truth and that Christians should seek for more enlightenment that is within the preview of reason.

In conclusion, Niebuhr believes that no one model or paradox should be taken as the typology of ethics to ascertain or generalize Christian principles rather it should be a guide to understanding the way we all individually come to know Christ through our personal faith works. As Niebuhr, puts it simply:

"The Christ who speaks to me without authorities and witnesses is not an actual Christ; he is no Jesus Christ of history. He may be nothing more than the projection of my wish or my compulsion; as, on the other hand, the Christ about whom I hear only through witnesses and never meet in my personal history is never Christ for me. We must make our individual decisions in our existential situation, but we do not make them individually in confrontation by a solitary Christ and as solitary selves."

5.1.2. EXERCISE 1

To sharpen your skill in analyzing and evaluating the content of a text by way of critically reflecting on your experience, retuning to events in your life that can apply the ideas of the book or that you may not apply same. How questions?

1. How does this book work in my context?
2. How does this new idea compare to my previous theological knowledge?
3. How does this new idea/knowledge change or not change your theology?

What Questions:

1. What are the expectations that you begin with?
2. What religious new faith practices do you most want to explore and describe?
3. What types of changes will take place with your new knowledge?
4. What religious practices of your context do you seek to query? Give the rationale for it?
5. What is the intervention you will carry out based on your new knowledge?

5.1.3. How to Think Theologically, Howard W. Stone and James O. Duke. Fortress Press, Minneapolis, 2013.

Rev. Awele Ilobah, Dish (Ed), LLB (Law), MA. (HRM), MA. (DIV) Doctorate Candidate, Hadin Simmons Theological Seminary, San Antonio, Texas.

Review Year

Spring 2017, DMIN.

Authors Intention

Stone and Duke want their readers to know that doing theology proper involves a good assessment that takes into consideration starting from the standpoint of examining the scripture and tradition and then look at its social implications that are embedded within the context in which the interpreter operates. The author's aim is to help readers to understand that theology cannot be done in insulation outside of its culture.

Keywords

Embedded theology- Deliberate theology-Interpretation -Correlation -Assessing- Tradition Reason- Reflection -Sequential and parallel synthesis.

Thesis Claim

Howard and Duke claims that thinking theologically is a process of thinking about life in light of the faith that Christians engaged in as a response to their calling.

Introduction

Howard W. Stone is a professor emeritus of pastoral theology and pastoral counseling at Brite Divinity School, who has written several inspirational books on pastoral counseling. His writing has covered topics on brief pastoral counseling, crisis counseling, depression, and hope.

James O. Duke is the Wylie Elizabeth M Briscoe Professor of History of Christianity thought in Brite Divinity School. His scholarship is known throughout European and American religious studies. One of the best works is *Makers of Christian Theology in America* (1997).[28]

Stone and Duke's book *How to Think Theologically* puts forward a view of theology as seeking after understanding. Thinking theologically is a process of thinking about life in light of the faith that Christians engaged in as a response to their calling.[29] Theology is about God, faith, and belief; Theology is concerned with how we come to know the truth about God. Thus, the Christian faith is an embedded theology that is rooted in its language. For example, theological language can be found in praying, hymens, singing, liturgy, and social action. Also Stone and Duke describe two kinds of theology: embedded theology, which is an inherited faith that has been passed down, and deliberative theology, which is a careful reflection on our embedded theological conditions. In doing theology proper, one has to reflect on his/her embedded theology in light of his/her deliberate theology. In addition, deliberate theology is our ability to evaluate relevant data, testimonies, and ancient and historical writings so that we can have an adequate understanding of our faith. As Christians, we are called to increase our growth in faith, which is the re-enforcement of our understanding of faith.

---

28 Howard W. Stone and James O.Duke, *How to think Theologically*, (Fortress Press, Minneapolis, 2013),xi.

29 James B. Nickoloff, Gustavo Gutierrez: Essential Writings (New York: Orbis Books, 2000), 32-33. Sees theology as a critical reflection in the light of God's world, its ultimate norm of judgment comes from revealed truth of what we accept by faith (inherited believe) not be reality. Also see Bernard J.F. Lonergen, *Methods in Theology*, (New York: The Seabury Press, 1972), 3. Lonerger defines theology as the ability to intellectually understand faith. For him intelligent takes more than human experience and to be intelligent means to ask questions what, how and why something came to be the way it is.

As Christians, our theology is fashioned in three ways:

- The interpretation of the meaning of the Christian faith from the perspective of the Christian message.
- The correlation of the theological interpretation with other interpretations, i.e., the task of relating theology to the circumstance of their lives.
- Assessing the adequacy of the interpretations and their correlations by looking at different worldview religions that are proposed by various philosophers. This has to do with our moral judgment. For example, one might evaluate theology's appropriation of tradition, reason, moral integrity, and validity.

In addition, Stone and Duke list four ways that we can reflect on theology proper. These are through

- Tradition: it helps us to guard against being caught up in the implicit theologies of present churches or doctrinal practices.
- Reason: it helps us to make sound, clear and coherent, and well-informed judgments about a belief.
- Experience: it helps us to draw from our past; it is about something that took place in our lives.
- Reflection: it helps us to design the message of God in our present context.

Stone and Duke are of the view that theology is culturally located within every context. Thus, a good assessment will take into consideration and start from the standpoint of examining the scripture and tradition and then look at its social implications that are embedded within the context. Furthermore, when doing theology, a Christian believer has to be creative in their reflection as well as being critical. For example, the processing can be done by applying the theological method of sequential thinking, i.e. thinking that has progression. It can be measured and analyzed. Another theological method of thinking is parallel synthetic thinking. This is the thinking that processes information all at once. Although Stone and Duke highlighted the importance of both methods of thinking as being proper in assessing theology, they advise that sequential and parallel synthesis have to be verified by sharing our thoughts with others and by listening deeply to God, friends, and our family.

According to Stone and Duke, theological reflection is an imaginative, creative, craft-like enterprise. A proper assessment of theology will help an individual to make sound theological judgments. For example, it can help a Christian make explicit the theological understanding of the Christian message. It can help Christians to examine those understanding by knowing their strengths and limitations, it can help to propose what seems to be the most adequate resolution to the issues in light of the scripture, and it helps to explain various conflicting theological terms.

In summary, for Stone and Duke, no theology operates in a vacuum but within a given community at a historical point in time. Also, it is the accent of the people (community/Church) that gives theology its meaning. Meaning theology is whatever the people assent to in the light of their understanding of the Gospel. Thus, the Church is the custodian of the Gospel and its gatekeeper. The gospel should be regarded as the touchstone for all Christians. It is the core of meaning behind the Christian faith. It shapes what we do and how we see life. For Stone and Duke, the Gospel is used by Christians to speak to the essentials of the Christian message of God.

Stone and Duke holds the view that the meaning of theology is derived from the assent of the community (church). For example, early Christians tried to define their identity in relation to their heritage in Judaism, and all questions pertaining to faith were interpreted from the law book and scriptures. And the question of life was also interpreted from the scripture and tradition during their time.

It makes the writer wonder the implication of this stance of theological interpretation in light of the struggles and pain that are present in our contemporary human society. For example, Stone and Duke talk about the human condition, the social dynamics of the human person, and issues concerning sin and sin-related questions. An example is what to do with gay, lesbian, or bisexual members of a church, and how the church should deal with such issues in light of the present interpretations in the scriptures.

I hold that when dealing with such social issues as homosexuality, same-sex marriage, and gender-identity crisis, with the application of the Stone and Duke model of interpretation, a minister will have to make use of the sequential and parallel synthesis model of interpretation, and they will have to give interpretation to the rightness or correctness of the issues by resorting to scripture, tradition, reason, experience and a psychological counseling research model.

For instance, studies have shown that a person's sexuality is deeply tied to their self-identity. The issue of self-identity has long being tied historically to gender specifics; our gender determines a lot who we are and what group we belong to. As such, because our personal experiences and worldview are colored by our upbringing, culture, family background, and even our faith system, this will affect the way a minister will practice ministry and counseling. Thus, different ministers will give different interpretations because of the differences in their worldview, and the answers given will be different from case to case.

In addition, since our sexual identity is deeply tied to our self-identity, meaning God created us to be of a particular sex and made us in his image. In the doctrine of the creation story in the book of Genesis, it is said that God created them male and female, and in his image he created them. So, sexuality and self-identity, as far as using scripture as a source for our critical reflection, will be accepted as being interconnected and not separated.

Reason and history, however, tells us that sexuality is biological. Such evaluation is regarded as scientific since its truth can only be found in nature. This makes me wonder how Stone and Duke's method of assessment will be useful in determining the truth. The truth as we know it is culturally relative, and as such what can be moral right in one culture may not be moral right in another culture. In the light of this hypothetical case scenario, the question is whether our sexual identity is a part of our genetic make-up or if it is developed as a result of the choices we make. Some studies have claimed that it is genetic, and this school of thought is of the view that it is in the human genetic makeup, and another group seems to link the cause to environmental factors such as peer groups, lifestyle, urbanization, and the worldview of the current day and age.

It is my view, having made recourse to experience, that there seems to be no conclusive evidence that our sexual orientation is connected to the biological makeup of humans or that we are born to be homosexual. The most likely thing, over the years, is that such behavior is a result of social factors. For an effective assessment of how to do theology properly regarding issues of sexual identity crisis, the minister will have to seek answers outside the traditional four sources: tradition, reason, history, and experience. A good way will be seeking expert advice or making use of therapeutic skills in dealing with such questions. One of such methods will be to look at the family system theory makeup of the congregant or member that is seeking help. Here the minister has to determine what the values and belief systems of the congregant are and what the values and belief system of a minister is regarding self-identity and sexuality. For example, the values system of some congregants may be that they believe that their sexuality is tied to his faith. To this group of people, it is clear that their spirituality is important for them to accept their identity and find themselves. They may hold the view that scripture states that that God created every one of us as perfect beings and in his image he created us. And they may also draw from the lesson of Peter;

nothing created by God should be called unclean because it does not fit the cultural expectation. Thus, there are several verses in the Scripture that speak about our sexuality, some supporting sexuality as being linked to procreation and as such reflecting God's purpose of creation and others that offer no evidential proof of its permissibility in the scriptures. The scripture holds strongly against homosexuality. Both scripture and tradition expressively condemn homosexual action or behavior. But if the methodology that Stone and Duke suggest should be applied in pastoral care, how do we counsel our congregants or members that are struggling with a daughter or a son that suddenly declared that they are no longer heterosexual but homosexual? For me, I find Stone and Duke's suggestion on the application of reason that is both parallel and sequential as being theoretical and not practicable. First, if a shepherd applies these two theological methods of assessing, reason will suggest that the scripture always speaks of the Christ-for-culture therapeutic paradox model or Christ-against-culture paradox, meaning the theology that is fighting against the culture. Whatsoever model the minister will use in his application will be based on the actual practices and beliefs of his/her community. What assent does his/her church gives to such issues of faith and this truth will have to be spoken in love.

Thus, the societal expectations of the community are then linked to the nominal cultures that are in operation within the social context, and since the church is a part of that social context, whatever is prevalent within that culture will be the norm that will be followed.

Another example: if such issues are raised in a Western community of faith, there will be some people that will put away tradition and scripture and uphold same-sex unions, not because they are bad and unchristian but because the cultural norm to accept such behaviors as being valid. On the other hand, if such issues are raised in an Africa context, they are brought down without hesitation, because such ideas are foreign to the cultural norm of the people. Base on this fact, it is arguable that the very fact that we can reflect theologically on matters of faith does not necessarily mean that our actions will be altered by the new theological awareness that we have come to realize since we are still operating within a particular context. Our actions and behaviors will remain unchanged when we do not feel safe in the environment for us to be ourselves. Thus, a person can only carry out their informed judgment as long as the operating context supports it since he/she does not operate in isolation but lives within a community. As a minister working within a contemporary society in the 21st century, what this means for me and other ministers is that our goal is to help people accept these implications. By this I mean to help them accept sexual identity synthesis and hold to their own evaluative framework.[30] By so doing, the person will be best able to evaluate and overcome the sexual identity crisis later in life. Furthermore, as a minister, I have to meet the people where they are and help them to cope with the anxiety that they are facing. For example, I may choose to use the Christ and culture in paradox model, which is a model that looks at the tension between our relationship with Christ and the person to who Christ has called us to be.

I will also have to keep in mind that I may not be able to apply the same principles to every case because each individual case will differ from person to person and from culture to culture. As such, as a minister, I have to more open and flexible to the possibilities that the focus and outcome of the counseling may not be for the congregant to embrace their sexuality, but it may be the case that they seek to be able to accept their identity. Also, the relationship of my value framework and the congregants has to be taken into consideration, the status of the value framework and the goal of the counseling, whether the congregant is seeking help for spiritual direction in their life or whether they are mainly struggling with some psychological issues relating to

---

30 Yarhouse, M. A., & Tan, E. S. N *Sexual identity synthesis: Attributions, meaning making, and the search for congruence.* (New York: University Press, 2004), 106,107&122.

their sexual orientation. All these have to be taking into consideration before healthy counseling is given. As a minister, I have to always be aware of the fact that we are all made up as creatures of nature and in the image of God. Human beings function as holistic beings composing of a body, soul, and spirit. All components function separately but form a unified entity in resemblance to Trinitarian God, but not with the same perfect nature with God.

In addition, as human beings, we are fallible creatures who long for salvation and the grace of God. Based on this fact, I have to be empathetic to the fact that we are human creatures and at the same time spiritual beings. They need to able to listen to what God is doing in the congregant's life. Also, I must help them find their place in God without seeking to change them but seeking to walk with them as they discover what God's plan is for their life without compromising the truth of the Gospel.

5.1.4. EXERCISE 2

To sharpen your skill in analyzing and evaluating the content of a text by way of critically reflecting on your experience, retuning to events in your life that can apply the ideas of the book or that you may not apply same.

1. As you reflect on the content of the material do you find yourself more engaged with the material as being applicable to your context?
2. What positive aspects of the material are applicable to your context? And how would you make use of the new knowledge? What aspect of the material do you struggle with?

BIBLIOGRAPHY

A, M. Yarhouse, & N.S. E.Tan, Sexual identity synthesis: Attributions, meaning making and the search for congruence. New York: University Press, 2004

Lonergen, Bernard J.F. Methods in Theology. New York: The Seabury Press, 1972.

Nickoloff, James B. Gustavo Gutierrez: Essential Writings. New York: Orbis Books, 2000.

Stone, Howard W, and James O.Duke, How to Think Theologically. Fortress Press, Minneapolis, 2013.

5.1.5. The Pursuit of God. A.W. Tozer. Michigan, Baker Publishing Group, 2013.31

Rev. Awele Ilobah, Dish (Ed), LLB (Law), MA. (HRM).
Graduate School of Theology, Abilene Christian University, Abilene, Texas.

Review Year
Fall 2016, MDIV.

Authors Intention
Tozer seeks to ignite a deep refining fire for God in the mind of the modern generation which he fears has lost the ideal of cultivating and exercising spiritual gifts. His aim is to help theological students and bible teachers on how to help their community of faith do theology proper in the face of changing circumstances in the world that threatens their faith.

Keywords
Faith in operation- Self -Submission-Trinitarian Relationship – Long Seeking- Soul Paradox-optic veil of the Self- Self-life-self–righteousness-self–love-self-contemptuous-self-pity-self-confidence-self-admiration.

Thesis Claim
When believers give a total submission of themselves to God, it helps to open their minds to be more receptive of the Divine and his economic plan for the salvation for Humankind. This brings about the renewal of the heart and helps humans to develop a personal relationship with God.

Introduction
Tozer takes spirituality to a whole new level with his book, *The Pursuit of God*. In his ten provocative essays, Tozer sees spiritual discipline to

---

31   A.W. Tozer, The Pursuit of God (Michigan: Baker Publishing Group, 2013), 1.

be something that is not achieved by our personal effort but rather it is something that is brought about through the grace of the Holy Spirit. For him, spiritual growth is self-submission to the powers of the Holy Spirit.[32]

Tozer draws his inspiration deeply from the scriptures. For him, the Bible is not to be taken as the totality of knowing the person of God that has ceased to be active in the present time, but rather the Bible should be seen as God's continuous speech. It is a means of drawing believers to the internal knowledge of God through their personal experience with the Divine. This knowing he described as the mind's way of having mental sexual intercourse with the Divine. Involving in spiritual activities disciplines of the body will help the mind create intimate communions with the Divine before a healthy relationship is created. For him, the ultimate purpose for the creation of all humans is to know God and his son Jesus Christ whom he has sent. This he calls "eternal life."[33]

We experience, therefore, eternal life here on earth, not after death.[34] This means God is present here on earth and can only be found by those who diligently seek him; the whole economy of salvation is for God to bring us into a right relationship with him and bringing back the original creator-creature relationship that God shared with humans at the garden of Eden. For Tozer, the manifestation of the reality of God's presence can only be known when the believer is aware of him.[35] When believers give a total submission of themselves, i.e. the body, soul, and mind to God, it helps to open their minds to be more receptive to the

---

32 Schwanda, Tom. 2007. "Christ plays in ten thousand places: a conversation in spiritual theology." *Christian Education Journal* 4, no. 2: 444-447. *ATLA Religion Database with ATLASerials*, EBSCO*host* (accessed August 5, 2016).

33 Philip Sheldrake, Spirituality: A Brief History. (Chichester: John Wiley & Sons, 2013), 7-8.

34 Greenman, Jeffrey & George Kalantzis. Life in the Spirit: Spiritual Formation in Theological Perspective. (Illinois: IVP Academic, 2010), 50-51.

35 Philip Sheldrake, 19.

personhood and the wonders of God in creation. God's essence begins to renew the mind, thereby lifting up the mind to a contemplative state where it begins to see himself/herself, creation (community) in relativity with the Divine plan. The believer begins to love God for what He is. He/She joins in a sacred Trinitarian relationship; each one depending on the other to fulfill God's greatest plan for humankind.[36] This Trinitarian relationship reveals Christ's plan in Creation, in the history of salvation, and in community.[37]

According to Tozer, this plan calls for an active involvement of a Christian. He/She becomes active in a participative life of faith, whereby Christians prove their love for God by the everyday choices they make. Christians believers should know that they must make a decision to follow God, the whole person (body, soul, and mind) needs to be involved in this following, this Tozer calls "life in the spirit," a higher kind of life which calls for an unconscious submission of the whole person under the power and anointing of Holy Spirit. The Holy Spirit is a life-giving spirit that resides inside of everyman. When parts of the human body are open unto the Spirit, the body becomes healthy and is united with the Holy Spirit. Where this transformation is properly achieved, the Christian believer ceases to be called a spectator in the world, but they are called to be in active partnership with the Divine in carrying out the creation plan. Therefore, believers are co-creators whose purposes are not meant to only create on earth, but whose duty is to care for the things that God has created and called into existence.[38] God calls

---

36 Colm Luibheid, *John Casssian Conferences: Translation and Preface* (Paulist Press: New York, 1985), 102-103. "Therefore, if we wish our prayers to reach upward to the heaven and beyond we must ensure that our mind is cleared of every earthly defect and cleansed of all passion's grip and is so light of itself that its prayer, free of sin's weighty load, will rise upward to God.

37 Ibid, 102-103.

38 John J. Collins. *Introduction to the Hebrew Bible* (Minneapolis: Fortress Press, 2014), 80-82.

believers into a life of faith to his table to share his body and drink his blood. Thus, at his table we are all equal partakers; there are no class, gender, culture, and race differences. For the Father seeks all believers to worship him in spirit and in truth, He welcomes everyone who truly seeks Him wholeheartedly to join in an active participation without any feeling of a disjointed and highly specialized doctrinal culture that is found among contemporary churches.

God becomes the believer's central point of existence from which he/she owes their very existence; however, Tozer warns that this awareness of the soul of the presence of God cannot be reached just by self-effort because it is a gift given by God, a gift of faith that must be recognized and cultivated if it is to grow and be sustained. Faith in operation becomes central to the believer's pursuit of God.

Tozer defined this kind of faith as a continuous gazing of the soul upon a saving Trinitarian God. For him, a heart held steadfast on God develops an inward secrete communion with God, which creates an intimate relationship.[39]

In addition, Tozer described the relationship between the human soul and the Divine as one that has to do with the soul paradox of love for God, which results in an active desire to find God and needlessly pursue after him through disciplines of worship, seeking, and searching by means of praying, fasting, contemplation and solitude. For him, it is only a soul that honestly seeks and zealously pursues God that finds him. Tozer prefers to use the term **long seeking** because the primary focus of his book is to help those who truly taste after the righteousness of God. These he called "those who are mighty longing about God." For him, there must be a holy desire of God in the heart of believers. Tozer seeks to ignite a deep refining fire for God in the mind of the modern generation which he fears has lost the ideal of cultivation and

---

39 Greenman, Jeffrey & George Kalantzis. Life in the Spirit: Spiritual Formation in Theological Perspective. (Illinois: IVP Academic, 2010), 24-25.

exercising spiritual gifts. For him, this modern generation only knows God in pieces. But for Tozer, God cannot be known in pieces. A person that seeks should seek him with his whole being—the body, soul, and mind. Thus, the only thing that keeps man away from the enjoyment of this reality is the optic veil of the "Self".

According to Tozer, this veil hinders us from salvation. These he describes this as the "Self-life" which he listed as self–righteousness, self–love, self-contemptuous, self-pity, self-confidence, and self-admiration. These he considered to be the treasure of the world. For him, our real treasure should be inward and nurtured by God. For a soul that finds God has everything and a soul without God is robbed of the sweetness of a romantic mental intercourse with the Divine. Such a soul has missed the very sweetness of love, which God offers to every person that finds him. That person has missed the very purpose for which they were created, which is to know God and be reunited with him in holy splendor.

5.1.6. EXERCISE 3

To sharpen your skill in analyzing and evaluating the content of a text by way of critically reflecting on your experience, retuning to events in your life that can apply the ideas of the book or that you may not apply same.

How questions?

1. How does this book work in my context?
2. How does this new idea compare to my previous theological knowledge?
3. How does this new idea/knowledge change or not change your theology?

What Questions:

1. What are the expectations that you begin with?
2. What religious new faith practices do you most want to explore and describe?
3. What types of changes will take place with your new knowledge?
4. What religious practices of your context do you seek to query? Give the rationale for the choice you make?
5. What is the intervention you will carry out based on your new knowledge?

BIBLIOGRAPHY

Collins, John J. *Introduction to the Hebrew Bible.* Minneapolis: Fortress Press, 2014.

Greenman, Jeffrey & George Kalantzis. Life in the Spirit: Spiritual Formation in Theological Perspective. Illinois: IVP Academic, 2010.

Luibheid, Colm. *John Cassian Conferences: Translation and Preface.* Paulist Press: New York, 1985.

Schwanda, Tom. "Christ plays in ten thousand places: a conversation in spiritual theology." *Christian Education Journal* 4, no. 2 (September 2007): 444-447. *ATLA Religion Database with ATLASerials*, EBSCO*host* (accessed August 5, 2016).

Sheldrake, Philip. Spirituality: A Brief History. Chichester: John Wiley & Sons, 2013.

Tozer.A.W. The *Pursuit of God*. Michigan: Baker Publishing Group, 2013.

5.1.7. Life of the Beloved: Spiritual living in a secular world, Henri J.M. Nouwen. New York, Crossroad Publishing Company, 1992.[40]

Rev. Awele Ilobah, Dish (Ed), LLB (Law), MA. (HRM), MA. (DIV) Doctorate Candidate, Hadin Simmons Theological Seminary, San Antonio, Texas.

Review Year
Spring 2017, MDIV.

Authors Intention
Nouwen intends to help baby boomers and non-religious believers who are struggling with discovering their giftedness in the world, being faced with judgmental guilt of church polities, religiosity of tradition within the churches. He wants them to know that there is a creator that exists in relativity to all things and that it is in sharing the self that humans come to become the best version of whom God has created them to be. He sees the love of thy neighbor that one comes to love God deeply.

Keywords
Fred-handicap -center of life-sacred life-unsacred world- control life-self's intrinsic - extrinsic nature- choosiness-becoming life-blessedness-holy sacrament -brokenness.

Thesis Claim
Nouwen claims man comes to the utilization of his/her full potentials once he becomes aware of his/her choosiness.

---

40   Henri J.M. Nouwen, *Life of the Beloved*: Spiritual living in a secular world (New York, Crossroad Publishing Company, 1992), 1.

Introduction

Nouwen speaks of spirituality on a whole new level in his book, *Life of the Beloved*: Spiritual living in a secular world, Nouwen sees spiritual life as a life that speaks to us about trust, hope, love and one that creates a vision for living in the secular world. Nouwen draws his inspiration from his deep friendship with his friend Fred and his community of faith where he worked with handicapped people. His reflection of life, humanity, and God were interring woven with these three worlds. For him, this relationship was a covenanted relationship that exists between humans and God.[41] It is a relationship that is tied to the center of the self, from where everything and everyone is connected.[42] This he called the center of the self, which he describes as a human's being's purpose for existence. Thus, human beings are relational beings, they are created to be in relationship with God, each other, and the things that God has created.[43]

Although Nouwen acknowledges the difficulties of living a sacred life in an unsacred world, the struggles that human beings face in coming to terms with their true human nature is the fact that humans are involved in an endless desires of our human heart quest for certainty and absolute control of life such as our desire to control time, power, pleasure and even death. In human's attempt to control life as we know it, humans

---

41 Colm Luibheid, *John Casssian Conferences: Translation and Preface* (Paulist Press: New York, 1985), 102-103. The believer begins to love God for what He is. He/She joins in a sacred Trinitarian relationship; each one depending on the other to fulfill God's greatest plan for humankind. This Trinitarian relationship reveals Christ's plan in Creation, in the history of salvation and in community.

42 Bruce D. Marshall, Trinity and Truth (Cambridge: Cambridge University Press, 2000), 113. "The Spirit role is to make all things come together. The Spirit gives all things their proper share in the divine life."

43 Philip Sheldrake, Spirituality: A Brief History. (Chichester: John Wiley & Sons, 2013), 7-8. Eternal life is the ultimate purpose of life. Living ultimately means to be in relationship with God through his son Jesus Christ and in relationship with created things.

become entrapped within an ever busyness of life, where the things which people desire the most now becomes the things that enslave them and make them unhappy. Nouwen feels these struggles can be overcome when humans chose to walk in the way of the beloved. Thus, the word "Beloved" was used by Nouwen as an expression of discovering the self's intrinsic and extrinsic nature as a "Being." That is made in the image and likeness of the creator.[44] This imaging and likeness of the creator are present in every human created by God. For him, man comes to the utilization of his/her full potentials once he becomes aware of his/her choosiness. Also, Nouwen believed that becoming the beloved requires an intentional living of life in the spirit. Spiritual life for Nouwen is a way of being and a way of becoming. The "being life" has to do with the awareness of the gifts that is indwell within us; this is the unique nature and gifts that we are born with, we know this gift, we don't learn them they just manifest some as talents and others as special abilities. And the "becoming life" he describes as the human way of discovering innate potentials, it is immaterial and cannot be seen because it has to do with the human spirit. Thus, becoming life has to do with the spirit's ability to search outside and beyond itself for virtues such as truth, love, beauty, and death. This virtuous are in of itself the essence of life, on them, the human existence lies. They reveal the ultimate reality of human life principles because they control what, who and why of everything we do i.e our actions and inactions. Also, they are the reason for human existence, in them lies the total economy of God's salvation plan. [45]

---

44 NIV.

45 John J. Collins. *Introduction to the Hebrew Bible* (Minneapolis: Fortress Press, 2014), 80-82. Humans are co-creators whose purposes are not meant to only create on earth. A.W. Tozer, The Pursuit of God (Michigan: Baker Publishing Group, 2013), chap. 7, (accessed December 30, 2016). Tozer calls this kind of life "life in the spirit," a higher kind of life which calls for an unconscious submission of the whole person (body, soul, and mind) under the power and anointing of Holy Spirit.

According to Nouwen, this kind of active life living is an expression of our beliefs and hope. This He class a life of faith, this kind of life can only be practice when humans begin to practice what they believe by continuous engagement and re-engagement with the created world. For Nouwen this is what the scripture means by eternal life, eternal life is found here on earth, it is an existential human experience and not an abstract intellectual mystical ideal, it is a reality because it is based on our daily experiences of life.[46]

Nouwen described this kind of faith becoming with the metaphorical image of the celebration and receiving of the Holy Sacrament. For him, there are four stages for identifying and becoming the beloved. Nouwen explains these four stages as representing the four stages of receiving the Eucharis, the Taking, the Blessing, the Broking, and the Giving of the Eucharist bread. The being "Taken" represents being chosen by God for a unique purpose on earth. We all have our individual uniqueness that is endowed on us by our creator, this uniqueness may sometimes bring hardship, challenges, and blessings, but being aware that we are chosen specially to be who we are, helps human's to operates within the chosen nature of their existence, it helps them to own it and by owing it, they can start using their unique gifts. Also, the opposite of this truth may lead one into a feeling of self-doubt, low self-esteem, and a state of self-rejection.

Secondly, Nouwen talks about the blessed stage as the stage where we are blessed through various acts of affirmation from family, friends, and community. For him, every human being longs for deep affection from one another. Also, affection can be received in the form of prayers and exhortation from our community of faith; it can be received by receiving and sharing of our presence. Here Nouwen talks about prayers and solitude as two forms of being blessed and living in the blessed life.

---

46 Greenman, Jeffrey & George Kalantzis. Life in the Spirit: Spiritual Formation in Theological Perspective. (Illinois: IVP Academic, 2010), 50-51.

He sees prayer as a way of listening to the blessing from the voice of the spirit, it is a silent act of listening deeply; it is a place where deep touches deep.[47] Nouwen a way of practicing this stage of blessedness is by interacting with the scripture text; memorizing the text in such ways that we know the words off by heart and the text become a part of our memory. This practice helps the human mind to be concentrated on the divine and protect the mind against the numerous distractions of the world around them.

In addition, Nouwen talks about the brokenness stage, he describes the stage of brokenness as the dark side of life, it is found in our struggles, pain, and suffering. For him this human brokenness is part of very fibers of the human existence and is experienced in our daily encounters and interactions with other humans and forces of nature, it is fully present and active within the human sphere of life. Nouwen sees "death" as an example of such brokenness, which he talks about. For him, even though with death comes pain, death should not be feared, rather it should be celebrated and embraced as a part of life. For him, brokenness is the full realization of our humanity. Nouwen talks about living the life of bro-kenness under the light of blessing in which a way that our brokenness makes us shine like diamonds, he quote a priest "we are diamonds once we are broken. Our beauty shines so bright and our through colors are seen." For him when we are broken, our life stories become hopes and strength for other people to follow.

Lastly, Nouwen talks about the given stage. For Nouwen, the given stage is the state where we share ourselves with others. It is a stage where the other three stages find their fulfillment. Thus, for him, we become

---

47   Benson, W. Bruce. 1988. "Working the Angles: The Shape of Pastoral Integrity." *Word & World* 8, no. 1: 92-94. *ATLA Religion Database with ATLASerials*, EBSCO*host* (accessed September 28, 2016). Bruce believes that the book of psalms prays for us when we interact with it. When believers read he psalm's during it helps them hear what God is saying to them. Also, prayers can be described as an antiphonal responds to the music of God.

beautiful people and live to our almost full realization potentials when we give what we can give. This can be in form of smile, handshake, a kiss, an embrace, a word of love, a present. Anything that is a part of our life to others, even the suffering that comes through the pain of death should be celebrated. Nouwens concludes that on these four stages lies our true happiness and actualization of full potential. Thus, it is in the realization of our God-given opportunities that we become who we are, to affirm our own true spiritual nature, claim our truth and reality of our being and chosen creatures uniquely created by God for his eternal purpose to be light of the world.

5.8. EXERCISE 4

To sharpen your skill in analyzing and evaluating the content of a text by way of critically reflecting on your experience, return to events in your life that can apply the ideas of the book or that you may not apply the same.

1. Does this text challenge you to rethink your belief, relationship, and practices in any way? Do you find yourself agreeing with the author by responding yes?
2. Does this new experience call for a change or modification of the relationship with people in your network?
3. Are you aware of the risks involved in adapting my faith by rationalizing and holding back from being judgmental?

BIBLIOGRAPHY

Benson, W. Bruce. 1988. "Working the Angles: The Shape of Pastoral Integrity." *Word & World* 8, no. 1: 92-94. *ATLA Religion Database with ATLASerials*, EBSCO*host* (accessed September 28, 2016).

Greenman, Jeffrey & George Kalantzis. Life in the Spirit: Spiritual Formation in Theological Perspective. Illinois: IVP Academic, 2010.

John J. Collins. *Introduction to the Hebrew Bible*. Minneapolis: Fortress Press, 2014.

Luibheid, Colm. *John Cassian Conferences: Translation and Preface*. Paulist Press: New York, 1985.

Marshal, Bruce D. l. Trinity and Truth. Cambridge: Cambridge University Press, 2000.

Nouwen, Henri J.M. *Life of the Beloved*: Spiritual living in a secular world (New York, Crossroad Publishing Company, 1992.

Sheldrake, Philip. Spirituality: A Brief History. Chichester: John Wiley & Sons, 2013.

Tozer.A.W. The *Pursuit of God*. Michigan: Baker Publishing Group, 2013.

5.2.0 Practical Theology: An Introduction, Richard R. Osmer. Michigan, William B Eerdmans, 2008.

Rev. Awele Ilobah, Dish (Ed), LLB (Law), MA. (HRM), MA. (DIV) Doctorate Candidate, Hadin Simmons Theological Seminary, San Antonio, Texas.

Review Year

Spring 2017, DMIN.

Authors Intention

Osmer's intention is to help equip congregational leaders to guide their communities with theological integrity and help ecclesiastical leaders to develop an indwelt knowledge of how to think and dialog theologically which he believes is lacking in the church today.

Keywords

Spirituality-Ethnographical Survey-Family system-Guided Interpretation-Priestly listening-Thoughtfulness-Theoretical Interpretation-Wise judgment-Self-differentiation

Thesis Claim

Osmer claims that doing theology proper involves four stages of asking and reconciling the following questions: what is going on? Why is that going on? what ought to be going on? How might we respond to it? And seeking answers to resolves the theological conflicts that arise from the investigation.

Introduction

Richard R Osmer is Thomas W. Synnott Professor of Christian Education at Princeton Theological Seminary. His scholarship includes A teachable Spirit and The Teaching Ministry of congregations. His book Practical Theology is unique in its attention to interdisciplinary issues and the ways that theological reflection is grounded in the spirituality of leaders and his intention is to help equip congregational leaders to guide their communities with theological integrity and help ecclesiastical leaders to develop an indwelt knowledge of how to think and dialog theologically this he believes is lacking in the church today.[48]

In *Practical Theology: An Introduction,* Richard R. Osmer, an expert in practical theology defines his view on thinking theologically in light of postmodern learned congregation and learned leadership. He urges his readers throughout his book to develop a healthy critical mind frame of thinking theologically. For him, thinking theologically involves four stages asking and reconciling the following questions in the light of what we are investigating or seeking answers for. First, learned leaders have to ask the following questions:

- What is going on?, this has to do with the descriptive empirical tasks of gathering information by reading beyond the face values of the case before us, looking intentional at the dynamic of the case by paying attention to social, political, economic, and cultural situation that is going on with every case.
- Why is that going on? this has to be with the interpretative task, here the leaned leader has to draw from reasons and empirical evidence to better understand the situation before him,
- What ought to be going on? this has to be with the normative task of interpretation, it seeks to answer the question by making recourse to experience, tradition and logic.
- How might we respond to it? this has to be with the pragmatic task, here the leaned leader will have to ask the question of what the new plan is, draw out implementation for the plan.

---

48 Richard R. Osmer, *Practical Theology: An Introduction,* (Michigan, William B Eerdmans, 2008), x.

According to Osmer, every human being has a narrative framework in which he/she sees and interacts with the world around them; this framework also sharpens our perception of things. For him, for a learned leader to be able to carry out an effective and sound theological interpretation, he/she has to first do what Osmer calls an ethnographical survey of the human person and individual we are dealing with to help us understand their history. For him, the key questions to ask when dealing carrying out an ethnography study is to carry out deep listening into their past, ask questions about their social and family context, one way he suggests is that the learned leader makes use of the Family system theory to identify the patient expression of pain. Also, the learned leaders have to trace the psychological line of interpretation. For instance, he/she can ask the question; what do we know about the patient emotional life? Are there any history or patterns that are unfolding? In addition, he/she has to look at the anthropology and cultural aspect of situations when carrying out theological assessment. For example, the learned leader can make recourse to scripture, reason, history, tradition, experience, and even ethical principles so as to arrive at a clear and sound answer that will be helpful for his learned congregation. [49]

Osmer classed the four tasks of practical theological interpretation which are Descriptive, interpretive, normative, and pragmatic into two, one of which he described as the thinking part and the other doing part. Thus, the thinking part of practical theology has to do with descriptive and interpretative because they involve actions that have to do with making use of empirical evidence, logic, reason, scientific and art resources. while the doing aspect, which has to do with the normative and pragmatic part of interpretation involves activities such as known practices, tradition, history, and human experience.

---

49 Howard W. Stone and James O.Duke, *How to think Theologically*, (Fortress Press, Minneapolis, 2013), 37.

Osmer sees practical theology as a web of life that is dynamic and holistic in nature; for him, theology cannot be done in isolation from culture. To do theology proper is to think and take action within a given context. Osmer, when doing theology proper, the learned leader has to think and operate within the interconnectedness, relationship, and system. Thus, since humans beings are created as substance dualism and operate as a holistic being, since every human being are an embedded web of nature and social system; during the period of crisis, it becomes important for a learned leader to pay attention to all relevant factors that may be relevant with that particular situation or case. Thus, it becomes necessary for the learned leader to see his/her congregation as a part of the community of interpretation that embodies a particular understanding of Christian tradition in its ritual actions, practices, and belief.

Following this line of thought, becomes important that the learned has several interpersonal skills, so He/ She can do proper interpretation. First, he/she is saddled with the responsibility of facilitating dialog between the interpretive activities that are already taking place and the interpretation generated by scripture, tradition, and other relevant sources. Also, he has to do what Osmer called guided interpretation; this has to do with knowing what practices are authentic and what practices are not. For Osmer, when doing theology proper, it is important for a learned leader to keep in mind what the goal is, and not to see it as an opportunity to manipulate people into doing what he/she wants or likes. Thus the goal here is to be able to provide the appropriate support, encouragement, and confrontation for your congregation by facilitating the dialog; this will involve consultation with people whose lives will be affected by the decisions and various stalk holders that will be involved with the implementation of the decision, the pragmatic aspect of the change.

The next is listening. There must be a practice of what Osmer called priestly listening, this involves bringing the situation before God in prayers by way of supplication, intercessory, and thanksgiving and lastly, there is the sharing between the people and the leader. Sharing has to do with invitation into each other lives and empathy. Also sharing may take the form of witness of preaching, here scripture can be brought in form of the local theology and folk art of the people so they can connect with the changes and are carried along. In addition, Osmer sees every research as having the following elements, i.e. the gathering of the information needed, this has to do with the empirical aspect of the interpretation, second the designing the method of gathering the information, next is the observation part, here you listen deeply and pay attention to details of the result that you are generating, application of the result.

Although Osmer in his first essay concentrated mainly on the various ways of doing theology proper. His second essay of his chapter two deals with the Osmer calls the interpretative task. For Osmer, a proper interpretation of the situation that going on will help the learned leader to understand and explain certain features of an episode situation or context, but it can never provide a perfect complete picture of the territory. Thus, an interpretative task will involve the leader's ability to develop an interpretative guide that will serve as a theoretical map in helping to navigate the people he/ she is leading to better make sense of their lives and the world around them as it pertains to God. Also, the Spirituality and maturity growth level of the leader is vital at this point. According to Osmer, there are three important components associated with carrying out an interpretative task. These are Thoughtfulness, Theoretical Interpretation, and wise judgment:

- Thoughtfulness: strives for insight into a particular circumstance of such people, which may even lead to kindness. Meaning empathy is the first step in an interpretative task. A learned leader should first put themselves in the shoes of the person going through the pain or in the situation.
- Theoretical interpretation: it involves the awareness that no one theology theory is perfect because theories come from construct knowledge of a particular perspective or position at a particular

time. As such no one perspective captures the fullness of truth, often many perspectives are needed to understand the multi-dimensions of a case, and this will differ from case to case. Also, Osmer points out the fact because theories are human-made, it is not free from error, mostly when it comes to the interpretation of things patterning and relating to God. For him, this is the distinction between the creator and the created for human knowledge about God is limited.

- Wise Judgment: This is necessary to determine when an action is courageous and not reckless and the available means to pursue courageous action in a given time and place. Also, it requires making the right choices since we are faced with several choices, knowing the good choice to make in every situation. The Bible says wisdom should be sort after because it is priceless, For example, the bible present Jesus as the wisdom incarnate who reveals God's secret wisdom. Jesus in his ministry seeks to manifest God's royal rule. Although Osmer sees these elements as being essential in carrying out theological tasks, it would have been helpful, and I believe a more robust idea if he included the cultural relevance of social norms and believes. Because according to him if theology is culturally relative within a particular time, place, and people. Therefore, it may mean that what one context or congregation regards as wise judgment will be different from what another congregation will regard as wise. If faith is a matter of belief and theology has to do with our beliefs in various faith principles; the theological interpretation should also be done within that context. If humans draw meaning from inherited folk tales and mythology, it means that all aspect of their interpretation will be done within that box, although one can argue that a leader can self-differentiate him/herself from being consumed by embedded culture but there is no guarantee, for our culture is a part of our lives, it is present from the time we are born to the time we die. We live and breathe culture and such our interpretation will stint by it.

Also, Osmer's conclusion for assessment in his case scenario on Olivia are all empirical and scientific, it is based on arts and science, he looks at various theories to arrive at his approach and on how to communicate with Olivia. He made mention of the cross-disciplinary dialog that leaned leaders should adopt but I like to add that as a more practical way, a leaned congregational leader can do since it is obvious that as a minister he/she will not have the time to invest in such critical dialog and research, a good practice will be to keep the contact numbers and network of several people in the science and art fields, by so doing when a situation comes up like Olivia case what he/she can do is to make a referrer or if the congregant does not want external contact then the minister leader can consult these experts for answers on what to do. I have found the later practice very valuable for my life and ministry that way I am not being harmful to the person who needs the help rather I am acting theologically.

5.2.1 EXERCISE 5

To sharpen your skill in analyzing and evaluating the content of a text by way of critically reflecting on your experience, retuning to events in your life that can apply the ideas of the book or that you may not apply same.

1. Do you find yourself saying "whereas now I think differently?
2. Does the new knowledge expose your assumptions and other factors you have taken for granted?
3. If you feel moved by the text what interventions are you willing to make in your personal life and in ministry?

BIBLIOGRAPHY

Osmer, Richard R. *Practical Theology: An Introduction.* Michigan, William B Eerdmans, 2008.

Stone, Howard W, and James O. Duke, *How to Think Theologically.* Fortress Press, Minneapolis, 2013.

5.2.2 Why Do Men Barbecue?: Recipes for Cultural Psychology. Richard A. Shweder. Cambridge, MA: Harvard University Press, 2003.

Rev. Awele Ilobah, Dish (Ed), LLB (Law), MA. (HRM).
Graduate School of Theology, Abilene Christian University, Abilene, Texas.

Review Year
Fall 2013, MDIV.

Authors Intention
Shweder wants his readers to be more enriched and informed about different cultural practices that exist in the world -by taking a look at their own worldview and adopting a more informed approach to engaging cultural differences and appreciating human commonality.

Keywords
Cultural Anthropology -Cross-cultural Comparison- Cultural -Female genital circumcision-Globalization

Thesis Claim
Shweder claims that the world should not be viewed only from one angle but from many angles in order for one to have an accurate perception and knowledge of what guides their moral judgment.

Introduction
In *Why Do Men Barbeque?* Richard Shweder, a cultural anthropologist and psychologist, defines his view of cultural psychology in light of postmodern humanism. He urges his readers throughout the book to reconsider their worldview when dealing with cultural practices and customs outside their context. He discusses in detail much of the cultural concept through various examples. Each example develops his central theme that the world should not be viewed only from one angle but from many

angles in order for one to have an accurate perception and knowledge of what guides their moral judgment.

Shweders's book is divided into three sections: first is the figuring of genders in different nations in Western and non-western cultures, the second section talks about representations and resistance, and the last section talks about global views and the subject of social changes. All three sections emphasize cultural relativism and pluralism. All eight essays provide new insight into colonialism as opposed to western civilization views. However, it could be argued that his essays do not speak about the effect of globalization and its economic changes despite the fact that these have contributed to significant changes in cultural perceptions.

His eight essays cover a variety of cultural issues and practices. For example, he addresses the different cultural backgrounds of co-sleeping parents and children. He draws a comparative analysis of the practice between Japanese, Indians, and Anglo-American middle class, concluding that no practice of any of these cultures is more superior to the rest. In that essay, he brings to light the emotional aspects of and the dangers inherent in making hasty generalizations about different cultural practices. He argues that an American who thinks that young children are not supposed to sleep with their adult parents or relative is actually culturally relative, and therefore different practices should be treated as contextual, and not to be regarded as repulsive or something bad.

Shweder calls on his readers and other anthropologists to hold the following proposition: our knowledge is incomplete if seen from one point of view but is incoherent if it is seen from all other cultural points of view, and yet should be regarded as void if it is not connected to any particular context. For him, a comprehensive and accurate way of interpreting culture is for one to keep in mind the tensions that arise from each culture and how best to engage it.

Shweder's most controversial and provocative essay covers the third world custom of female genital circumcision: regarded as disgusting by Western culture but held in high esteem by those who practice it. African women see this practice as being prestigious and a rite of passages, giving power and building pride in their heritage. Shweder makes an impassionate plea to his fellow anthropologists to embrace cultural pluralism when they encounter a different culture. He calls for tolerance and holds that much consideration be given to such practices.

Shweder uses a technique of cross-cultural comparison of different cultural practices and value expressions as a method to expand on what he considers to be the basic epistemological position in the study of cultural phenomena. He brilliantly avoids taking an absolute stand on moral imperialism and relativism. Rather, in his argument, he sustains a healthier evaluative stance by making inquiries into various social practices in a way that explores them further. Thus he avoids the pitfall of being guilty of making a hasty generalization about any of these practices. He does not claim absolute knowledge of the culture since he himself cannot be said to have given an authentic view of a culture, which he does not have a legitimate right to speak upon because he is an outsider. However, his approach opens the door for various models of interpretation in every case, thereby leaving his reader more enriched and informed by taking a look at their own worldview and adopting a more informed approach to engaging cultural differences.

In addition, it can be argued that his position creates a very compelling yet difficult approach to understanding the relationship between true knowledge of a thing which belongs to the realm of epistemology and our general perspective of a thing, which has to do with our interpretation of thing based on our moral judgments. To him, most people too often connect with postmodernism and his relative factors when engaging cultures. They fail to consider the contextual environment where the event is taking place to best understand and appreciate the practices and values of the people whose lives are being judged.

Again, Shweder makes the general claim that humans are often faced with challenges to deal with evolutionary psychology, notions that affect their emotions and clarify their morality lens. To him, such a psychological lens is not brought about by biological factors. Instead, they are brought about by social and environmental changes taking place around a person. One wonders what Shweder will have to say to the gay community which claims that their self-identity is tied to abnormal changes or defects in their biological makeup. It is difficult for the gay community to agree with Shweder's point of view that social and environmental factors control the practices and belief system of a place. Moreover, the fact that much of Shweder's work was centered on addressing contemporary issues of the 19th century, and given his evaluation theory, it is difficult for his critics to draw a conclusion that he was indirectly ranking one cultural practice from one culture above another culture since he talks much about tolerance and acceptance.

Finally, the essays encourage us to be slow to judge another's culture and to be more fully informed before taking a moral stance about other people that are different from us. Shweder invites us to engage and act as an informed cultural critic. He urges us to reject moral relativism but only after we have achieved an in-depth knowledge of local ethnographic realities of the people who live we intend to investigate.

5.2.3 EXERCISE 6

To sharpen your skill in analyzing and evaluating the content of a text by way of critically reflecting on your experience, retuning to events in your life that can apply the ideas of the book or that you may not apply same. Why questions?

1. How does this book work in my context?
2. How does this new idea compare to my previous theological knowledge?
3. How does this new idea/knowledge change or not change your theology?

What Questions:

1. What are the expectations that you begin with?
2. What types of changes will take place with your new knowledge?
3. What cultural practices of your context do you seek to query? Give the rationale for the choice you make?
4. What is the intervention you will carry out based on your new knowledge?

5.2.4 The McDonaldization of Society, George Ritzer, SAGE publications, Maryland, 2013.

Rev. Awele Ilobah, Dish (Ed), LLB (Law), MA. (HRM).
Graduate School of Theology, Abilene Christian University, Abilene, Texas.

Review Year
Summer 2016, MDIV.

Authors Intention
Ritzer wants his readers to know about the negative and positive effects of Globalization and its effect on lifestyle and culture.

Keywords
Globalization-Vertical McDonaldization -The Irrationality of rationality

Thesis Claim
Ritzer claims McDonaldization connects people's emotions and their rationality so people no longer think for themselves; rather, the mind is helped to think. This deception creates a false feeling of safety by making people to prefer the same product over and over again. Becoming homogenous creates a negative that begins to affect the ability of the human mind to be creative since their choices are limited.

Introduction
In his seven provocative essays on the McDonaldization of society, Ritzer argues that McDonaldization is an emerging value brought by social and economic development. He skillfully links McDonaldization to Weber's theory of rationality. According to this theory, in an attempt to have a perfect world, modern society employed the use of efficiency, predictably, calculability, and non-human technology, which controls people. Thus, Ritzer's essays can be viewed as an extension of Weber's theory of rationality, which is centered on the realm of consumption. His definition of McDonaldization does not present something new, but rather

is the culmination of a series of rationalization processes that had been occurring throughout the 20th century which humans were already used to. Thus, his extensive research on what he terms "McDonalidization" is just an elaborate form of the effect of globalization. For him, globalization is a trans-planetary process or set of processes involving increasing liquidity and the growing multidirectional flow of people, objects, places, and information and includes the structures people encounter and create that are barriers to or expedite those flows. Ritzer expounded on the constant flow of goods and services as being instrumental in the expansion of globalization. Although, one could argue that Ritzer urges his readers to face the threat of McDonaldization and globalization, especially the effects they have on human psychology and on the way we live our lives.

Ritzer analyzes his concept of McDonaldization by using mainly the fast-food restaurant process as an illustration and then comparing the different variables associated with the concept of globalization in western society. He emphasizes how changes in the economic power of nations affect the lifestyle and culture of people. Ritzer's analysis of McDonaldization, which centers mainly on fast-food restaurants, limits his methodology and his assessment. He can be said to be guilty of using a particular aspect of society to make a general claim about the whole. Thus, put simply using the cause and effect of a particular variable in a system to access the whole. Rather a healthier approach would have been for him to examine various variables outside the fast-food restaurant. For example, he may have given consideration to political and social factors like family dynamics and environmental factors that are contributing to the changes in the society. Instead of looking at the economic effects only, he should have looked at all the social factors that humans are engaged with, factors that affect the cultural life of the people.

Ritzer looked at the psychological damage caused by fast-food restaurants and chains and studied the impact they have on civilization. His most obvious examples of this kind of economic power are McDonald's, Burger King, Wendy's, and other upscale higher-priced chain restaurants like steakhouses, Chili's, Olive Garden, etc. He analyzed the effect of how the existing global market powers have used their businesses in the exploitation of Western society so they can make more profit. McDonaldization has not only changed the lifestyle of people but also affected the family dynamic and the mindset of an entire generation. Some of the examples that Ritzer gives of this effect can be seen in the extension of working hours, which is a shift beyond the normal cultural working hours. This extension has created a chain reaction of changes in the family dynamic. For example, because many families now spend longer hours working, parents spend less time at home with their children and the children lack the necessary home training they need to develop into well-formed responsible adults. Thus, in some cases, such children become a menace to society.

Ritzer also gives the example of what he calls vertical McDonaldization. This has to do with the monopolization of the market economy by multinational companies forcing smaller competitors out of business. They do this by expanding their operations nationally and internationally, thereby increasing their level of production in order to increase growth and control prices. Ritzer believes that this act of McDonaldization has been counter-productive to society because it reduces competition, and thereby increases the homogeneity of goods and services. This homogeneity hampers innovation and hinders creativity.

Ritzer points out that this lack of creativity is due to the fact that McDonaldization now controls all aspects of human life. He gives an example of the influence of McDonaldization created by drug stores, fashion houses, shoe companies, and, largest of all, the technological market, which he considers to be the largest tool used by McDonaldization for manipulation of the economy and the human mind. To Ritzer, the use of technology by these mega-companies has given McDonaldization its power of control. For instance, the use of technology makes it possible for goods and services to be easily accessible. With the effective utilization of time and money, these companies are best able to calculate the amount of time needed to produce their goods and services so as to increase the quantity of products and reduce the quality of the product.

Another factor that has fueled McDonaldization is the fact that goods and services can be predictable by their consumers. To Ritzer, McDonaldization companies use predictability of goods and services as a tool to control human behavior. McDonaldization connects people's emotions and their rationality so they can no longer think for themselves; rather, they are helped to think. McDonaldization creates a false feeling of safety by making people to prefer the same product over and over again. Thus, because every good and service becomes homogenous, the negative impact is that it starts affecting the ability of the human mind to be creative since their choices are limited.

Ritzer calls this way of thinking "the irrationality of rationality," which is created by the use of technology and advertising by mega-companies. This has led to the change of rational thinking culture and has created certain lifestyles that are now acceptable by society as value-added and meaningful to their existence. Again, this argument has some limitations because the homogeneity of goods and services is sometimes created by laws and by the government for political reasons. Take for example the current situation in Russian ban on import of food from Europe because of the sanction on it on Ukraine. Where there is such a ban, goods and services become homogenous: only Russian food is available, and the people have no other choice than to buy what is available to them. It will affect the lifestyle of the people and stuff creates a change in the culture.

Much of Ritzer's book consists of exemplary deployment of the concept of McDonaldization through a number of case studies drawn from various multinational and national fast-food companies. These demonstrate that much of the changes in the modern world that we see today are caused by the manipulations of these multinational companies. His meaningful scholarship exposes the dangers of this by highlighting the negative impacts of McDonaldization on the cultural life of the people. But he carefully does not reject the positive aspects of McDonaldization, which he sees as helping to advance and improve human life. For example, he discusses how modern methods of technology have helped to improve the health sector, such as the use of various non-human technologies in the delivery of babies, which has helped in increasing the birth-rate and reducing mortality. Based on this fact, Ritzer is of the view that McDonaldization and its products should not be regarded as totally harmful.

He provides helpful tips for his readers on how to escape the dangers of McDonaldization so as not be imprisoned by them. Some of the suggestions he makes were to get involved in games, rational activities that one does on his/her own, thinking, participating in group activities such as knitting, carving, joining small group forums where one can have intellectual conversation. He suggests that people avoid daily routine as much as possible, spend more time outdoors, and learn to use technology to their own advantage by spending less time on it and depending more on themselves. He made a laudable attempt here which is commendable, unlike other writers, to not only expose the effects of McDonaldization and the problems associated with it, took extra steps to guide his readers on how to best live and avoid the chaos that he sees.

In ministerial practice Ritzer's book has helped to sharpen my thinking and views about how the cultural life of a people is formed, it has exposed me to some of the economic factors that have contributed immensely to this change in culture. As an implication for mission, I believe his model will be helpful in church planting. It will guide a minister when planting a church to expand his worldview by carrying an ethnographical report on the anthropology of the place where he is ministry to. For example, a missionary pastor from America that moves to Africa for the mission will find it difficult to operate effectively if he does not consider how the economic factors of the place affect the way of life of the people. For instance, the city of Lagos, Nigeria, where I served as a missionary leader for seven months, is a highly industrialized place where people are off to work before 3 am and business begins, finishing by 10 pm, and in some areas, people work 24/7. The people have no time for themselves and a person's workplace is four hours from where they live. Thus, when my evangelism team goes out, everyone you meet does not reside in that area, and at the end of the day, they go back to their different residential homes. This makes it difficult to properly convert them into the household of God because of distance and you may not see a person you speak with next time. Again because of the business hours you cannot have a church gathering during business hours because nobody will attend the service. Thus, Ritzer's principle of McDonaldization helps me understand how the economic life of a place affects the life of the people so we have to give consideration to the economic lifestyle of the place when planning church programs and activities if we are to succeed.

5.2.5 EXERCISE 7

To sharpen your skill in analyzing and evaluating the content of a text by way of critically reflecting on your experience, retuning to events in your life that can apply the ideas of the book or that you may not apply same.

1. Does this text challenge you to rethink your belief, relationship, and practices in any way? Do you find yourself agreeing with the author by responding yes?
2. Does this new experience call for a change or modification of the relationship with people in your network?
3. Are you aware of the risks involved in adapting my faith by rationalizing and holding back from being judgmental?

What Questions:

1. What are the expectations that you begin with?
2. What types of changes will take place with your new knowledge?
3. What cultural practices of your context do you seek to query? Give the rationale for the choice you make?
4. What is the intervention you will carry out based on your new knowledge?

5.2.6 Spiritual Preparation for Christian Leadership, E.Glenn Hinson, UpperRoom Books, Nashville, 1999.

Rev. Awele Ilobah, Dish (Ed), LLB (Law), MA. (HRM), MA. (DIV) Doctorate Candidate, Hadin Simmons Theological Seminary, San Antonio, Texas.

Review Year
Summer 2017, DMIN.

Authors Intention
Hinson seeks to help modern-day evangelicals Christians to understand what the term biblical spirituality truly is. He hopes to help church leaders and congregants to put away the feel-good attitude of worship and to embark on encountering God on a deeper sacred level.

Keywords
Baby Boomer-Paying attention to God-Revival of the Soul-Messiah Trap-Sabbath

Thesis Claim
Hinson claims that a persons' desire to love God only comes when such a person is able to develop perfect affection for the divine.

Introduction
Glenn Hinson talks about Christian Spirituality from a different perspective in his book "Spiritual preparation for Christian leadership." Hinson in chapter one and chapter two lays out his thesis statement and helps his readers to understand why he wrote the book, for him, like many before him he is concerned about the circle perception of the word "spirituality" and how it is practice by modern-day evangelicals Christians. These people he referred to as "Baby Boomers" or "generation of seekers." Further, he described this set of believers as feeling

estranged from God, separated from each other, lacking meaning in life, void of roots, and a societal connection. Also, Hinson listed the five major characteristics of these Baby boomers as authenticity, community, lack of dogmatism, focus on the arts, and diversity. Thus, the Baby Boomers are actively involved in their own quest and prefer mystical religion because it is more open.[50] For this reason, Hinson is concerned about this kind of faith practice, and he is convinced that this kind of belief is dangerous to good spiritual growth.

Following this, in his essay in chapter three Hinson argues that the central concern of a Christian should be focused on having an intimate relationship with God. He/she should want to know God, they should have the desire to partake in the life of God and not just know about God. Also, Hinson highlighted that this kind of desire only comes when a believer begins to develop perfect affection for the divine. In other words, the believer begins to see God as his/her lord and personal savior. In fact, the believer accepts the Lord as the lover of his soul. Hinson, describe this process of loving as the stage where the believers heart is open and the love of God enters into his/her heart in such a way that he/she is mesmerized by the beauty and perfection of God to the extent that they come to desire God more than any other thing in the world. Also, this love of God when it enters the heart of the believer it will drive out fear and remove all anxiety.[51] Thus, to best illustrate his point Hinson uses the example of two lovers that are lost in love for each other and desires to be constantly with one another.

In addition, Hinson's central ideal in chapter three was on prayer. Here, he described prayer as an act of paying attention to God. Thus, for him, paying attention to God means invariably loving God. For me, this point is very powerful and insightful because as part of my personal

---

50   E. Glenn Hinson, *Spiritual Preparation for Christian Leadership* (Upper Room Books: Nashville, 1999), 7.
51   Ibid, 40.

spiritual discipline I devout myself to prayers by withdrawing from my daily activities so I can acknowledge the beauty and holiness of God. This practice for me is an act of reverence to God and I believe this is what Hinson means when he describes prayers as an act of paying attention to God. For to pay attention to someone or something a person has to stop whatever they are doing and gaze at the object of their reflection. In the same light when we pay attention to God, God becomes the sole object of our affection and the center of our being. Also, praying to God for me means that I have to acknowledge God in whatever I am doing whether I am sleeping, eating, and studying, or in my discussion. Also, another insightful ideal I learned from this book is what Hinson called the "divinization of all things" that God has created. Meaning there is a connection of God with everything created thing in the universe. Therefore, it follows that God uses the created thing of this world as being a channel through which God speaks to us. As Hinson puts it "All of life should be a prayer: if you knew how to look at life through God's eyes, if you knew how to listen to God in all of life he says all of life will become a prayer. A twenty-dollar bill, the sea, a pornographies magazine, a wire, a youth brought in with an overdose of drugs, a drunk in the middle of the street, a hospital everything, a prayer." Following this, Hinson concludes this chapter by rephrasing what he meant by "paying attention to God." For him paying attention requires deep listening and deep listening involves good listening. Thus, the following are the qualities that a good listener has vulnerability, acceptance, expectancy, and constancy.[52] Also, being a good listener requires a revival of the soul. Meaning the listener has to take time off to be in solitude and silence moments so he/she can connect with God. Here, Hinson advises his readers that a good way to be a good listener is by adopting a habit of creating space within the busyness of our life for reflection. Again, this last point is very important to me because as a practice I observe some

____

52 Ibid, 50.

of the elements he listed as the quality of a good listener. For example, like withdrawing from the busyness of life so I can reflect on myself or on my day's activities. I enjoy doing this whenever I am in the US, but once I touch the shores of Africa it is a different story. My work life is so great, and my involvement does not give me so much time and space to spend time in solitude because I am in a doctorate program, actively involved in the preaching and teaching ministry and carrying out evangelism in several villages and training ministers around the country and overseas via the internet. Some of my close friends and mentors have asked me how I manage to do these things and I have always said it is by the grace of God, but the reality is I pray to have rest, time to journal, and stay connected with God. This is why I love this aspect of listening mostly, where Hinson says that we should try to see God in everything. Although I must confess that his use of pornography magazine came as a shock to me because of my morality /ethical perspective and I am sure most ministers will react to this example in the same way or they may not react to it. But I wonder how male ministers guide their hearts from wandering into sin if they take pornographic magazine just to see the glory of God, what does the scripture say about our protecting our heart, so this is last point is a hard nut to crack. But I do understand what he is saying which is there exists a connection of all things with God. And this is true because there exists an element of divine presence of God in the created order of the universe whether human-made or by nature. As the bible stated that which the Lord has made clean we should not call unclean. This is a hard theology teaching and it is not for the faint-hearted. Moreover, in chapter 4 the Hinson speaks about how Christian leaders can hold themselves accountable for their actions. He gave several examples of how this can be done. One of the ways he mentions was, to begin with, the habit of Journaling as a form of spiritual practice. This practice involves spending time to reflect on our actions and life and writing it out in a form of a story. This helps us to keep track of the presence and actions of the spirit in our life. Again, in this chapter, I now know that it is important and a good practice to write down any revelatory dreams when we get up from sleep. However, I must confess that I sometimes have divine revelations that come to me in my dreams, but I am not in the habit of always writing it down and I think that should be something that I should start doing. Following this new knowledge after reading this chapter last week I had a read and I wrote it done on my personal journal. Furthermore, in chapter five Hinson talks about making the most of your Time; he sees this principle of keeping watch over how we use our time as a helpful practice. For him, we can overuse our time or underuse our time.[53] And either way is bad practice and dangerous to our spiritual life and our health. Thus, Hinson describes this kind of lifestyle as "Messiah Trap."[54] A good example of this habit is when a minister over labor himself/herself by trying to do everything and make everyone happy. And they end up burning out and not helping anybody. Again, as a confession, I am guilty of this practice or lifestyle and this is what I wrote in my learning covenant that I will like to be better at doing "Sabbath" quality time for myself and for my health and by God's grace, I shall make it. Thus, in Chapter six, Hinson takes his readers to the next stage where he talks about how a leader can maintain balance. Thus, for him, a healthy spiritual life requires a balance of experiential, intellectual, social, and institutional dimensions all of which help us to form a healthy relationship with God and with our neighbors. In addition, Hinson in chapter seven looks at sexuality and spirituality, and his quest in this essay was to answer the following key questions: How does sexuality affect your relationship with God? How does or should sexuality affect your relationship with other persons? How much sexuality contributes to spirituality? Here, Hinson talks about using our sex to glory God's purpose of creation and also about respecting our marriage partners. For him when it comes to sex and spirituality it simply means that we have a God that loves everyone irrespective of their sexuality and we who are created are meant to

---

53   Ibid, 77.
54   Ibid, 12.

approach God in holiness and in humility.[55] Furthermore, in chapter 8 he talks about how believers can sustain their spiritual life by reading, listening, and seeing. The goal here is attentiveness in everything you are doing, whether spending time with family, studying, preparing sermons, writing, visiting the sick in the hospital, leading worship, organizing and community activity, matching to protest injustice, or discharging many other tasks in which a responsible leader engages.[56] Also, Chapter Nine is a continuation of how a believer can continue to maintain his/her spiritual life by seeking solitude and silence times as a practice. According to him, spiritual life will not remain vital without solitude and silence. Solitude ends the ceaseless bombardment of your senses by external stimuli and permits you again to become collected. Solitude and silence is vital because it will require the believer to focus on God. Lastly, in chapter Ten Hinson again continues his essay on how to maintain and sustain the spiritual life by sharing the journey. He describes this process whereby a leader invites someone trusted into his or her life. Here, friendship and companionship is needed to sustain the leader during the time of struggles and pain. Thus, it is important that certain criteria are met before the leader can invite someone into their life to serve in that capacity. For example, such associates should be between the ages of the fourth plus and over, their sex matters because we are sexual beings and if they are of the same sex they will relate easily to what we are feeling. Experience is another key part, their personality, knowledge, humility and the situation matters too. Depending on whatever stage or the context of the situation the leader may find him or herself in will depend on what kind of friendship he will seek or whom to invite into his or her life.[57]

---

55   Ibid, 124.
56   Ibid, 135.
57   Ibid, 168-177.

5.2.7 EXERCISE 8

To sharpen your skill in analyzing and evaluating the content of a text by way of critically reflecting on your experience, retuning to events in your life that can apply the ideas of the book or that you may not apply same. Reflective questions:

1. What are the reflective expectations of how this book holds value to your life/ministry?
2. What types of changes will take place with your new knowledge?
3. What is the intervention you will carry out based on your new knowledge?
4. What is the disappointment(s) you may have with the premises outlined in the book?

5.2.8 An Altar in the World: A Geography of Faith, Barbara Brown Taylor, HarperCollins, New York, 2010.

Rev. Awele Ilobah, Dish (Ed), LLB (Law), MA. (HRM), MA. (DIV) Doctorate Candidate, Hadin Simmons Theological Seminary, San Antonio, Texas.

Review Year
Summer 2017, DMIN.

Author's Intention
Taylor wants her audience to understand that the secular world is a part of God's redemptive work and as such Christians need to recognize that taking care of the world around them involves being engaged within issues happening in the world. To her to do this is a part of God's redemptive purpose that everything He has created should be in a loving relationship with each other and with nature.

Keywords
Spirit- Character-Depth-Soil under her feet-The Spirit character and depth of a place-Land

Thesis Claim
Taylor's claim is that being a Christian does not mean that a person has to be disengaged from the secular culture and its activities because humans are not created to exist in isolation, but humans are created to be in relationship with everything that God has created.

Introduction
In *An Altar in the World: A Geography of Faith Barbara* Brown Taylor (whom many academicians and ministers consider to be a gift to the Christian church.) This focuses on spiritual practices and understanding of God in the sacred and secular worlds. At the beginning of the book,

she discusses the spiritual way of how to do pastoral care within a minister's context. The title suggests, "in my experience, every place has its own spirit, its own character and depth."

Reading that title captivated my heart immediately and struck a chord of cultural ethnography in my ministry context. These three words: spirit, character, and depth when used in relation to inanimate objects, brings them to life. For example, when Taylor describes the Hawaiian Islands she uses metaphors to personify the object of her affection and the world around her. Her writing is thought-provoking and inspiring at the same time. She observes every detail of the place and she relates it to her feelings, which become her experience. She personifies the object like the "soil under her feet" and makes it come alive like a living thing. There is a continuous communication and engagement with the "Land," which she calls the "spirit of the place." She connects the rest of the chapter to the Biblical story of Jacob and his eschatological vision of God. To Taylor, Jacob engaged with God by building an Altar so he could stay connected with the place where God appeared to him. The place where God appeared to Jacob becomes significant to Taylor in her attempt to help Christians understand that there is still the presence of God at work in the secular worlds and as such we should not avoid engaging the world around us. To her as a Christian, our light is meant to shine in the world and not to be hidden. For her, God is still as present and as active today as he was in ancient times.

She advises her readers to have a healthy relationship with God by not placing limitations on Him, for this is the only way for us to truly encounter Him. As I am reflecting on this point, I will say that in my ministry context I have encountered many times in my life when I had to deal with situations and with people who felt that Christians should have nothing to do with the secular world. These people believe that God should be worshiped within the church only and, as the Bible says we are not part of the world; we should have nothing to do with it. For me, I have found that God is in a relationship with everything that He has created. Even the secular world is a part of God's redemptive work and as such, we need to recognize this redemptive purpose of God by embracing the secular culture and the world because the world does not exist in isolation. There are people living in the world and when we disengaged ourselves from them, we disengaged ourselves from the world, and this cannot be part of God's redemptive plan since Jesus commissioned us as disciples to go into the world and make disciples of all nations even to the ends of the earth. This Great commission we cannot accomplish in isolation, but we can fulfill it if only when we fully engage the world and recognize that it is not our place to save the world, but salvation comes from God who only is the Judge.

5.2.9 EXERCISE 9

To sharpen your skill in analyzing and evaluating the content of a text by way of critically reflecting on your experience, retuning to events in your life that can apply the ideas of the book or that you may not apply same. What Questions:

1. What are the reflective expectations of how this book holds value to your life/ministry?
2. What types of changes will take place with your new knowledge?
3. What is the intervention you will carry out based on your new knowledge?
4. What is the disappointment(s) you may have with the premises outlined in the book?

5.3.0 Pastoral Theology: Essentials of Ministry, Oden, and Thomas. New York: Harper One, 1983.

Rev. Awele Ilobah, Dish (Ed), LLB (Law), MA. (HRM), MA. (DIV) Doctorate Candidate, Hadin Simmons Theological Seminary, San Antonio, Texas.

Review Year
Fall 2017, DMIN.

Author's Intention
The primary intent of his book is a classical ecumenism call with primary attention to the Christian ecumenical consensus of these centuries and its consequences to contemporary faith practices of today

Keywords
Modern-day Churches -Biblical gifting- Pastoral visitation-Theodicy for pastoral care

Thesis Claim
Oden starts that pastoral theology pays attention to integration of reason, tradition, and history of the church and personal experience which he calls systematic theology.

Introduction
Thomas C Oden is a Henry Anson Professor of Theology at Drew University. Also, he is an ordained minister and the author of fourteen highly respected and acclaimed books: *Game Free Agenda for Theology*, *Kerygma and Counseling*, and *Pastoral Theology: Essentials of Ministry*. But it is in this later book, *Pastoral Theology*, that he developed a more robust classical model view that is compactable with contemporary Christian practice. Thus, the primary intent of his book is a classical ecumenism call with primary attention to the Christian ecumenical consensus of

these centuries and its consequences to contemporary faith practices of today. Oden begins his introductory section by laying out what he believes to be the foundational knowledge of the pastoral office and its prerequisite for ordination. He starts by defining pastoral theology as a branch of Christian theology that deals with the consequences of God self-disclosure in history, and what the role, duties, and work of a pastor is. Also, his book draws attention to the integration of pastoral theology, social theology, liberation theology, and ethical theology in light of the practice of ministry. In other words, Pastoral theology has to do with the integration of theology and practice. According to Oden, pastoral theology pays attention to the integration of reason, tradition, and history of the church and personal experience which he calls systematic theology (ix-xi).

Furthermore, in Chapter one, he talks about how the changing effects of society have come to change the way ministry is done in the 21st century, citing examples of issues of women in ministry. He applauds this new move of the church to accommodate women by giving them pastoral and leadership roles, because according to him biblical tradition and history talks about several women in the bible who were disciples of Christ and also followers of Paul, and these women were not given any leadership recognized roles by the authors of the bible due to the biblical culture. Although these women were very significant in the roles and duties that they performed in the early church, they are not still recognized and appreciated in the life of the church today.

In addition, he sees pastoral theology as taking a new form in the future, and this new adaptation will greatly expand the ministry of the church mostly with dealing with changing events and predicament that are taking place in society today. But, Oden warns that the church should be careful in its adoption and acceptance of social and liberation theology. According to him, the church should not be too willing to change church doctrinal principles by over accepting and accommodating changing social events into the church practices for the sake of being tolerant, because these will make it derail from true apostolic teachings and tradition. For this reason, Oden advises ordinary people who desire to enter into ministry that they should first begin by asking themselves this question: why do ministry? Thus, to help readers understand what he means by this question, he begins by giving the definition of ministry. For him, ministry helps to shape the body of Christ. Also, in ministry, we are entrusted to bear witness to God's disclosure and actions in the world by this he means it is in the practices of our faith that we come to experience God. Also, God does not exist because we do ministry; rather, ministry exists because God exists, and God desires us to do ministry. (13)

Also, in Chapter two he lays down the key criteria for doing ministry is first that one has to have a personal conviction that one is called, being committed to lay down one's life. Next, having the gift and talent of preaching includes the power of persuasion and the rhetoric that is involved in its performance (19). Also, there should be a pre-ordination committee that will enter into intercessory prayers for the candidate; such a committee should test competence level. Lastly, he/she should have some formal training. Although the last view tends to be logical and is now practiced by most modern-day churches, this writer disagrees with it based on the fact that she is from an uneducated community in Africa, where Christianity is experiencing its largest expansion that the world has ever seen being carried out by uneducated men and women. Also, history has evidence that the majority of Jesus' disciples were only fishermen, but God used them (25).

Furthermore, in Chapter three Oden talks about the significance of ordination as being a public testimony and assented to by the church. Then, in Chapter four, Oden returns to the notion of women in ministry and comments on the harsh and wrongful interpretation of the role of women by modern-day evangelicals. For him, there is a valued Christological significance for the role of women in the church, and if anyone is looking for answers, they need not look further than considering the significance of Baptism because in baptism, everyone is received into the household of God and redeemed by grace, irrespective of his or her gender, and they are all called children of God. (38) Next, in Chapter five he makes an analogy between the role of the pastor as being like that of a shepherd; for him all ministry roles irrespective of their title bear resemblance to the role of a shepherd. As such in ministry, we are called to serve and tend the flock of God. (52-54) Hence, it is essential that the pastor possess certain skills that are vital in caring for the parishioners. Since humans are holistic in nature, it means that when caring for the parishioner, it involves caring for their physical, emotional and spiritual needs, (56-60). In addition, in Chapter six, Oden talks about the importance of Biblical gifting and offices; for him, all biblical gifting such as prophecy, miracles, and ecstatic utterances should be used for the edification of the community and should be practiced in accordance with the scripture. Also, all pastoral offices should follow scripturally laid down principles. He concludes this chapter by adding that teaching should be an intricate part of all ministerial offices irrespective of one's title; they are all required to go into the world and preach /teach the good news of the gospel, (76-80). Furthermore, Chapter seven talks about the pastor's role in leading the community in worship so that they can be sanctified, purified, and petitions can be brought before the Lord. For him, the contemporary pastor now bears the role of both the prophet and also functions as a priest. This, to him, is good practice even though in biblical tradition the priest is set aside and purified to take up such a role. As such, because of this change, Oden advises the contemporary preacher to get themselves familiar with the apostolic languages and liturgies used for worship so as to fully fulfill such a role by carrying out the proper function. He gives an example of how the apostolic liturgies used in ancient times in Baptism and Eucharist are still used by the modern churches, (86-100). In other words, it is not surprising that in Chapters eight and nine Oden talks more about the significance of the sacraments as being essential and central to Christ's ministry. For him, the wine and bread and water baptism are all visible presences of

God in the midst of the community. Also, he gives an example of how during the Eucharist the bread is broken into fractions, thanks is given, and it is shared with the congregation; he sees this practice as symbolic and representing how Christ shared his body for the world. (113-125)

Oden shifts his readers' attention to what he considers to be the essentials of good preaching in his essay. First, he defines preaching as the sharing of the good news about God to hearers (parishioners), and the Holy Spirit works through the word that is preached to bring about change in the believer's life. Thus, it is the Holy Spirit that gives the preacher the words to say. After the preacher prays, meditates, and seeks God's face during sermon preparation, the Holy Spirit takes charge of his/her body to deliver the message. In other words, for there to be a positive change, the preacher must be able to say what the Spirit has put in his heart. He emphasizes that preachers should be bold to speak the truth to the people without holding back or diluting the message of the text. (129-139)

Furthermore, in Chapter Ten of the essay, he talks about the church as being a learning community where parishioners come to learn so that they can grow spiritually in their faith work. As such, it is the duty and responsibility of the pastor to design programs that will help facilitate the growth of the community and so that members of the community can become all that God intends for them to be. (146-151) Hence, Chapter eleven talks about the role of the church administrator role as one who is responsible for the day-to-day running and operations of the church activities and programs. He /she should be one with skills that can easily improvise and adjust to changing circumstances in order to meet the needs of the church. (156-164) Still more, in Chapter twelve, Oden talks about the importance of pastoral visitation in ministry. Here, it is essential for the visitation of parishioners during times of sickness to be private; it should be in the form of a dialog between a pastor and the person in need. In addition, Chapter thirteen takes his readers deeper into what he sees as the pastoral care role of the pastor. For him, since humans possess body, soul, and mind. In pastoral care, the pastor is called to take care of the soul of the sick patient. Here, he/ she is required to pay attention by listening deeply to how the patient is feeling and what their needs are, being empathic to their pain, and having a self-knowledge of who they are, It is also important to have a clinical knowledge of what kind of illness that the patient is going through. Thus, the pastor should know that they are there to give hope and help the patient cope with the situation by strengthening their parishioner's faith. (192-202) Hence, in Chapter fifteen, Oden talks about the Theodicy for pastoral care; here he encourages the pastors on how they can help their parishioners cope with suffering and pain. For him, there is a formative power of suffering on the believer's spiritual life, because suffering helps us to purify, cleanses, and makes us chaste. (231) Also, he talks about how the pastor can help his parishioners relate to their condition as being temporal and not forever because as Christians we have an eternal hope to be reunited with God one day, and as such whatever pain we suffer in the physical only affects our mortal bodies. And when we suffer, we should remember that Christ also suffered and died for us, (245). Consequently, in Chapter sixteen, Oden emphasizes the pastor's role in times of suffering; here the pastor is advised on how he/she can offer counseling to the sick so that they can make sense of their condition in light of the love of God, as such when offering pastoral care to a sick person, the pastor should not go in to preach or read a lengthy sermon. Rather, it should consist of simple prayer, a short visit, and the language should fit the occasion for both the patient and the members of their family. (255-263) Thus, in Chapter seventeen Oden takes this principle of offering pastoral counseling further to the ministry of offering care to the poor. He advises that offerings, tithes, and funds should be raised to support and care for the poor in the church. Also, he sees the care of the poor as being the duty of every member of the church and as signifying caring for one's neighbor. (282-283) Lastly, in Chapter eighteen, Oden talks about the pastoral care of the dying. Here, he explains that during the time of death people do not need doctrine or doctors; all they need is for the pastor to guide their passing souls into the hands of God. So during the time of death, the pastor can sing, pray, give Eucharist, and console the family of the dying person. (299-303) Although this writer agrees with Thomas Oden's theology, and she sees it as being heavily drawn from apostolic tradition and biblical teaching, the following are likely questions raised from her reflection after reading the book. What is the importance of this book to this class and why was it chosen for this class? Secondly, what is the relationship between contemporary theology to the scripture and church fathers?, How does the publish date of this book (1983) relate to theology done in 2017? And lastly, where do Oden's ideals fit in pastoral theology, and can it be used more effectively in 2017?

5.3.1 EXERCISE 10

To sharpen your skill in analyzing and evaluating the content of a text by way of critically reflecting on your experience, retuning to events in your life that can apply the ideas of the book or that you may not apply same.

1. Does this text challenge you to rethink your belief, relationship, and practices in any way? Do you find yourself agreeing with the author by responding yes?
2. Does this new experience call for a change or modification of the relationship with people in your network?
3. Are you aware of the risks involved in adapting my faith by rationalizing and holding back from being judgmental?

What Questions:

1. What are the expectations that you begin with?
2. What types of changes will take place with your new knowledge?
3. What cultural practices of your context do you seek to query? Give the rationale for the choice you make.
4. What is the intervention you will carry out based on your new knowledge?

5.3.2 For All The Saints: Evangelical Theology and Christian Spirituality, Timothy George & Alister McGrath, Westminster John Knox Press, Louisville, 2003.

Rev. Awele Ilobah, Dish (Ed), LLB (Law), MA. (HRM), MA. (DIV) Doctorate Candidate, Hadin Simmons Theological Seminary, San Antonio, Texas.

Review Year

Summer 2017, DMIN.

Author's Intention

McGrath wants his readers to know that God as a loving created the world in Love and it was out of love that He revealed Himself to humanity through His son Jesus Christ. For him, humans can achieve their full potential of gifted when they are in complete obedience to the will of God and living their lives in accordance with His will.

Keywords

Paradigmatically-Perfectbeing-internalization-Trinitarian-Enhancing-Encountering

Thesis Claim

McGrath claims Evangelical spirituality begins with a deep knowing of God, it is the internalization of faith that saturates every aspect of believer's lives.

Introduction

According to Timothy George and Alister McGrath in their work For All the Saints: Evangelical Theology and Christian Spirituality; Evangelical spirituality is for all the saint-that is it is for all who know Jesus Christ and wish to make known to others the divine truth about God. Thus, the authors' thesis statements are as follows: How do evangelicals express the co-inherence of intellect and piety? How do they bring together the head, heart, and hands in a way that honors the instincts of their heritage while appropriating the spiritual treasures of the wider Christian tradition? And lastly, what is the implication of an evangelical spiritual theology for ethics and worship as well as for the teaching and preaching of mission in the church today? [58]

Consequently, when it comes to the evangelical understanding of spirituality it begins with a deep knowing of God, it is the internalization of faith that saturates every aspect of believer's lives. Thus, it is faith in operation that helps us in the understanding of the personhood of God, and by this I mean it begins with understanding of the Trinitarian God of love and grace. Therefore, it follows that the doctrine of the Trinity is a necessary framework for understanding the story of Jesus Christ as the story of God. Thus, since God is a spirit and a personal reality and power. As such, it follows that those who worship him must worship him in truth and in spirit. Also, God is a paradigmatically unbodily perfect being. And the scripture states that everything comes from God and depends on God. Thus, in spirituality, we are reminded that God created the world out of love because it was through an act of love that He revealed Himself in the world through the person of Christ who himself being God became our redeemer, reconciler, and savior. [59]

Also, spirituality is about being all that God wants us to be, it is about complete obedience to the will of God and living our lives in accordance with His will. In other words, spiritual formation is a long-time journey that ends with a complete rest with the Creator. Thus, we know that we are strangers in this world, and we all await a glorious splendor that has been prepared for us in heaven, and earth is not our home rather heaven is our final destination. For this reason, George &

---

58   Timothy George and Alister McGrath, For *All The Saints: Evangelical Theology and Christian Spirituality (Westminster John Knox Press: Louisville, 2003), 1–2.*
59   Ibid, 39.

Mcgrath points out to their readers in chapter one that the aim of the scripture is to change lives. According to the authors, theology should not be taken solely as being just a way to know God; meaning something that affects the way we think but it should be taken as something that affects the way we feel and ultimately how we live our lives.[60] Thus, this belief is rooted in the Christian theology of faith that holds that spirituality has to do with faith in operation. And this kind of faith is seen as an active kind of faith that makes the believer cease to spectators, but active participants of what God is doing in the world. Obviously, a faith in operation begins with the knowledge of God intellectually and the experiencing of God.[61] Christian spiritual formation can be described as the point where deep touches deep. There the believers come to live a life of more authentic faith, In other words, the Christian individual aim to deepen their experience of God or to practice a deep relationship with God. For example, in my personal work with Christ, I have found the practice of contemplation to be helpful, although I must confess that it is sometimes difficult to stay still and focus for longer hours contemplating about God and allowing the center of my soul to connect with the center of life which is God, after reading this book it is my plan to try to connect more with my center by learning and practicing how to free my mind from the busyness of the day so I can focus deeply and connect my body, soul and mind to the Spirit.

Furthermore, the authors want their readers to know that all spirituality is about a personal appropriation of what of theology signpost and promises in the Scriptures. Consequently, the Bible should not be taken to be an ideological concept, but a living instructional manual that should guard our life because it is the living Word of God that gives life to all who believe in Him. Unfortunately, modern-day evangelicals have come to regard theology as solely intellectual intricacies that

---

60 Ibid, 11.
61 Ibid, 13.

have nothing to do with the way we feel and how we behave. Although both authors do not agree with this later view for them theology has to do with the love of man for God, confession, and repentance with the ultimate goal being a call for a change of behavior. Thus, regarding the last point, I do believe it to be the gospel truth. Because as a minister it is my view that the word theology encompasses everything related and pertaining to God that includes writings of the fathers, scripture, history and tradition (doctrine of the church), and our personal experience. Evidently, it means that a believer's understanding of God extends beyond the intellectual process, but it is such that includes personal feelings and emotions. Consequently, as human beings, when it comes to knowing God we come to know God with our whole person, namely, our body, soul, and mind that is subjected to the power of the Holy Spirit. In other words, spiritual practices or discipline of the body such as act of ceaseless prayer, meditation, contemplation, fasting, confession, solitude, simplicity, etc. helps to bring the human body into intimate communion with the divine before a healthy Triune relationship is created.[62] Also, it is my personal view that because we all are sinners and I need grace, and because we are still in this world even though we are not of this world. Thus, it becomes important that Christian believers come to the recognition of the fact that Christian spiritual formation is a process. In fact, it is a lifetime journey and it is not achieved by personal effort or by how intelligent we are or by personal achievement. Rather, it is something that is freely given and received by believers from the Holy Spirit through an act of grace. And just as the scripture says we are all sinners I need of grace and all have sinned and come short of the glory of God. Also, in another verse, it says even though when we were, yet sinners Christ loved us and died for our sins. Following this point, in chapter two George and McGrath, described spirituality as a formative process in which we uncover our inner lives to seek emancipation from

---

62 Ibid, 19.

our narcissism. In other words, the spiritual growth process can take the following stages of progression:

- What I ought to know? (This has to do with the intellect; it has to do with the theological knowledge about God. The authors called this process the enhancing our Appreciation. Thus, enhancing our appreciation has to do with the opening of the mind to avocation and devotion to God's divine essence).
- What I ought to do? (This has to do with encountering our emotions and feelings that move us into action. Thus, it is in this stage that the Christian believer comes to know the richness, wonder, and Joy of the simple word of forgiveness and repentance).

And what I ought to be? (This has to do with the Trinitarian relationship that reveals God's ultimate plan of salvation. Here, the believer begins to love God for what He is, he/she joins in a sacred Trinitarian relationship; each one depending on the other to fulfill God's greatest plan for Humankind.[63] This Trinitarian relationship reveals Christ's plan both in Creation, in the history of salvation and community.[64]

Furthermore, in chapter 3 the authors take their readers into a whole new phase on how a Christian believer can be formed spiritually it is this part that I feel that my congregation will benefit from because it speaks about the end product of being spiritually formed is that we should be light in the community. Also, it is about being in a relationship with God. More so, according to the authors, spiritual

---

63 Colm Luibheid, *John Casssian Conferences: Translation and Preface* (Paulist Press: New York, 1985), 102-103. "Therefore if we wish our prayers to reach upward to the heaven and beyond we must ensure that our mind is cleared of every earthly defect and cleansed of all passion's grip and is so light of itself that its prayer, free of sin's weighty load, will rise upward to God.

64 Timothy George and Alister McGrath, 1-2.

formation in Christ is for the whole life and whole person. To be spiritually formed means the sharping of our spirit towards union and action with a triune God. Therefore, Believers are co-creators whose purposes are not meant to only create on earth, but whose duty is to care for the things, which God has created and called into exist-ence.[65] Again, Spiritual formation refers to the process of sharping our spirit to conform to the spirit of God. Thus, the believer there-fore enters into partnership with God as a co-creator rather than spectators. Hallelujah, Hallelujah this is where I feel the church is lacking today, particularly in my church there are so many believers who feel that they understand God enough and already knows him and have spiritual gifting, these set of people wants to micro-manage everything. In fact, they love everything the church is doing they can give little of their wealth, but they don't want to serve, they believe service is for the Priest. They can give their money to feed the poor or clothe the homeless but they will not go to the homeless, I honestly think my congregation needs to hear that the ultimate aim of spiritual formation has to do with our involvement and partnership out there in the community, not the community of God because they already know God but the community of the world which we should be in active partnership with God and being salt and light of the world. I hope to start up a discipleship spiritual program that talks about service as one of the formative gifting of the Holy Spirit so that my congregation can be filled and blessed by God.

Finally, in chapter 6 of the book, the authors talk about a clear cut between the life of the flesh and the life of the spirit. According to the authors, the life a life of the spirit means to be in union with God and to be in participation with the divine life. Therefore, for this reason, God is constantly seeking to create a radical redemptive community of believers whose benefits are not meant primarily for themselves, but for God and

---

65 Timothy George, 45-46.

the world.[66] It is this last point that I personally find to be very important and beneficial for me, my congregation in Africa, and Christian ministry in the world. The writer believes that at the center point of every believer or human's there is the divine presence of God. Thus, for me, God can be found in every human being that he has created and as Apostle Paul rightly puts it in the Lord we move and have our being and in Him, we hope for our existence. If this is true it follows that God becomes the believer's center point of existence from which he/she owes their very existence. Also, it is because of this truth that the soul of humans seeks for eternity and our human desires are endless and until we find our rest in the Creator the soul runs empty and remains far from its center (God). This is the reason why it is very important for every believer to seek the pursuit of spiritual precepts and spiritual gifting; it is my belief that this is the primary purpose of the book which is the book was written for those souls who have a mighty longing for holy desire for God. Furthermore, it has come to my knowledge that as a Minister it is very important that my congregation learns to love and desire the knowledge of God more than anything else. Our love of God should not be just because of what we have received from Him, but because of who God is. For this reason, it is important that my church organizes spiritual retreats and seminars that help the congregation to develop and grow in various spiritual disciplines such as fasting, daily reading of the Bible, memorization of scripture etc. Although, I do agree with the author's view that there is a trend in the West that shows that there is an endless pursuit of intellectual knowledge that is devoid of personal experience with the Holy Spirit. For in the pursuit of spiritual precept one should not allow him/herself to have too much engagement in knowledge to the extent that one is disordered from experiencing the divine truth, thereby making the acquisition of knowledge dangerous if its sole purpose is not to glorify God. But I do not agree that problem in

---

66 Ibid,105.

the Western Christian or with most believers emanate from the lack of understanding about God, but that the problem arises from the fact that Western believers or some educated believers concentrate so much on the intellectual aspect of the knowledge about God why there is little or no actual practice of the experience of the spirit. My reason being since we humans are designed to be spiritual beings that are made of a body, mind, soul, and body. It is only reasonable that we also come to experience God with all our wholeness and not just with the intellect. Because God is a supernatural being and he is an emotional being, and also a spirit being. We who come to come to God must connect with him in the center of our soul where the spirit is located. As such, it becomes proper that modern-day believers should not only seek spiritual precepts as just kind of new knowledge, something new to add to their basket of knowledge. But spiritual precepts should be sought through the self – disciplines or practices that awakens the soul and pulls the spirit to a deeper relationship with God. And the final result of a healthy spiritual practice will lead a Christian believer to develop a love for God. [67] In conclusion, as part of my learning growth and implementation plan for my ministry I will keep in mind that spirituality is a part of God's plan for creation and that it is meant for all human beings both believers and unbelievers. Secondly, as part of the missioner leaders of my ministry, I will constantly remind my people of the importance of staying connected to God and the spiritual reward of it which is to know God. Also, I will be careful and advise my people to be mindful to think of ourselves higher than people who do not practice any spiritual disciplines as being lower or less aware of God, but rather my advise because as the authors agreed spirituality is for all people and God wants his children to walk in the spirit with him. Romans 8: 6 "The Spirit himself testifies with our spirit that we are God's children."

---

67   Ibid, 106.

5.3.3 EXERCISE 11

To sharpen your skill in analyzing and evaluating the content of a text by way of critically reflecting on your experience, retuning to events in your life that can apply the ideas of the book or that you may not apply same. Reflective questions:

1. Does this new knowledge challenge me to rethink my belief and faith practices in any way? Do I find myself agreeing or disagreeing with the concepts it shares?
2. Does this new knowledge call for medication of my previous understanding discipleship?
3. As I make this adoption and embraces the new knowledge do find myself more engaged with the principles set out in the book?

5.3.4 Prayer: Finding the Hearts True Home, Richard Foster. HarperCollins, San Francisco, 1992.

*Rev. Awele Ilobah, Dish (Ed), LLB (Law), MA. (HRM), MA. (DIV)
Doctorate Candidate, Hadin Simmons Theological Seminary, San Antonio, Texas.*

Review Year

Summer 2017, DMIN.

Author's Intention

Fosters' main ideal is focused on helping believers to discover how a person can develop affectionate love towards God, how to develop the spirit of endurance, and how to grow in faith.

Keywords

Simple prayer-Prayer for the forsaking- Unceasing prayer-Prayer action-Prayer of Complaint- Praying the ordinary-Meditational prayer- Breath prayer -Healing prayer- Radical prayer-Holy boldness- Holy habit-Holy distrust

Thesis Claim

Foster believes that prayer is the fundamental key to discovering who God is and that a person can come to take on a life of holy living by actively committing him/herself to an active continuous life of prayer.

Introduction

Richard Foster opens his book with the thesis statement that "True whole prayer is nothing but love."[68] Here, foster describes the love of God as that which draws a believer inwardly so that he/she may be

---

68   Foster Richard, Prayer: Finding the heart's True Home (San Francisco: HarperCollins, 1992), 1.

transformed. Also, this love takes the believer upward so that the soul begins to gaze upon the beauty of the divine to the extent that God becomes the center of the soul. Therefore, God becomes the center point from which the human spirit is aligned with the spirit of God. Also, it is at this point that the human spirit finds its resting place. In other words, God's divine spirit takes a believer inwardly so that His self-revelatory power can transform and awakens the soul and the soul becomes open to the divine essence of God. Basically, at the end of the process, the soul then takes on an outward-looking faith into the world. At this point, the believer becomes a blessing to the world. He/she enters into a Trinitarian partnership with the divine and becomes a co-caretaker of everything that God has created. Here, he/she becomes the embodiment of the incarnate Christ. They become the mind of Christ that brings healing to the world by caring for the sick, the hands of Christ that feed the poor and clothe the naked, and the heart of Christ that is compassionate to the sorrows and pain of a broken world. Evidently, Foster believes that the only way a person can come to take on this kind of holy living is to be actively committed to a life of prayer. Consequently, Foster sees prayer as the key to the door and this door is Christ. Moreover, Foster sees love as being at the heart of every prayer, besides it was out of love that Jesus offered Himself as a sacrifice so that all may be united with the father and it was out of this same love that God sent his only son to the world to die for our sins. As such Christ becomes the only way to our eternal destiny. Thus, the main idea of Foster's book is to focus on how believers can create a love relationship with God, how to develop the spirit of endurance, and how to grow in faith. For him, love is the essence of prayer and real prayer comes from pure love. Moreover, this kind of love brings the heart to a point of simplicity of healing so that the heart becomes captured into the hands of God. Here, we allow ourselves to be gathered into the hands of God so that he can transform, heal and use us for his glory.

Furthermore, Foster invites his readers into the world of prayer, and he opens his book by listing various forms of prayer that has been useful to him in his spiritual journey with God. First, is *simple prayer* this kind of prayer is not something that we come to master because to pray means to be willing to be a novice. In other words, we start by praying about small things. For him, there is no perfect prayer because when it comes to prayer like every other thing in life we become good at it when we practice it all the time. Naturally, the more we practice how to pray, we become better at praying. Thus, in prayer, there is a progression we begin from the beginner stage and we progress to a master stage. In other words, we grow from the simple to the complex. Also, Foster describes simple prayer as the kind of prayer where we learn to pray like little children.

Here, we can start with learning how to pray about our essential physical needs or by praying about little things. By this I mean we start by praying about little things that are bordering us. Also, we learn how to surrender all that we are and all that we have into the hands of God. Thus, we surrender control by rendering or submitting ourselves under the power of the Holy Spirit. In conclusion, my personal motivation for chosen to write on the simple prayer is because I am someone who works very hard, and I am very determined to get things done perfectly, and not only that I am committed to doing things the right way. Obviously, it is easy for me to apply this same strong work ethic to prayer. By this I mean I may fall into the trap of convincing myself that every petition I bring before my Father in heaven must be seen as something serious or class as a big problem. Honestly, I think this is what Foster is guiding his readers against which is that prayer should flow from the heart and it is not necessary for us to plan our prayers. Also, prayer can be a spontaneous response, not stressful, and not perfect. Thus, Fosters advises his readers to bring even the smallest things of our daily encounters into the father so that he can heal us and give us peace. For him, in prayer, we should learn to come to God just as we are. We must learn to bring before God all the good, bad, and ugly aspects of our lives. Just like Fosters writes simple prayer involves ordinary people bringing ordinary prayers before God.

Equally important, Fosters gave his readers some practical steps to begin with when learning to pray the simple prayer. First, they start with praying for friends, family, and neighbors. Second, we come just as we are before God without pretense. Third, we must never be discouraged. Next, we must let go of trying too hard. Finally, we must learn to pray even when we are dwelling in evil.

Next, is the *prayer for the forsaken*, Foster describes this kind of prayer as a prayer that is made when we feel abandoned, disappointed, and frustrated because we no longer can hear or see anything from God. Here, we begin to feel that God is absent and we hope to hear from him and we do everything and anything within our power and wisdom that is humanly possible to comprehend, but at the end of it all God seem so far away from us and there is no answer from God.

Again, my personal motivation for selecting this prayer is because I have said this kind of prayer at one point in my life, in fact, I can remember saying the prayer of the forsaking eight years ago my family lost my sister who died suddenly. Then I can remember feeling forsaken by God, it was just as Foster described it in this book. I felt God has abandoned my family. And not just that I begin to convince myself that maybe I have done something wrong against God and this is the reason why God was not answering me. I began to ask God why he did not save her; I said to myself it was unfair for this to happen to her because she was a good person. Truly, it was a feeling of dryness and loneliness and indeed there was an absence of God in my life that lasted for five years.

Although I was actively involved in ministry to the sick, the hungry and doing missions work in the villages, but I did not get an answer there was silence, but I kept on moving and following him. Honestly, I believe this is what Foster means when he advises that we should not think of ourselves as failures or as sinners, but that we should be reminded that even Christ himself felt this way when He cried out on the cross saying "My God, my God why have thou forsaken me."[69] Foster quotes that some historical scholars have described these dark moments as the dark night of the soul. It is a time when the soul cannot see beyond itself and it longs to hear from his one true love (God). Here, Foster advises his readers not to give up, but that they should continue to pray and trust in God. More importantly, Foster helps his readers to realize that darkness is a part of God's plan. Meaning darkness should be embraced and accepted as a part of life because we are all on a journey. Further, he describes this stage as a time when believers enter into a deep relationship with God because their faith has been tested and tried in such a way that soul is pulled towards God. For me, this is exactly what happened to me during my family bereavement. As the years go by I begin to discover God's infinite mercies and tender love towards my family and me. Also, the more I discovered this truth I let go of all my fears and doubts and this truth drew me closer to God. As for me, this period is a time when we develop true intimacy with the Father because at this point we feel vulnerable and lost because all our hope is gone and there is nothing or nobody to turn to. Thus, when this happens we discover that God begins to reveal his infinite perfect love to us. Again, it is at this point that we begin to see the beauty and goodness of God in everything he has created.

Again, according to Foster, there are two kind of silence that occurs during the forsaken prayer stage. First, we become deadened to any impression of worldly things or religious responses because it will all mean nothing to us. At this point, we no longer desire anything or bind ourselves to any condition, but we come to desire something new as we become willing to give up our "will" and submit ourselves under the power of the Holy Spirit. Here, we discovered that we could no longer

---

69 NIV.

manage God. Secondly, we are stripped off of everything we know and everything we believe, and as such, we become less of the center of our lives. Also, in this stage we begin to search for meaning, we wonder what kind of God, God is, and we come to what Foster calls a Holy distrust of God. Again, my personal motivation here is that I have come to discover that our inner person is broken open and we become focused on God because it is when we are focused that the soul is connected to God.

Following this is the *prayer of complaint.* Here, the petitioner feels forsaken, he/she goes into lament, but they have confidence in the reaction of God. Thus, they feel exasperated by the abandonment of God. Also, when making a prayer of complaint we continue to seek, ask and knock even though the doors are shut and we are overwhelmed by the predicament that has occurred. More likely we shake our fist at God and break into despise. Yet, we continue to seek, ask and search for answers even though there is no answer to our requests, but we are persistent in our commitment to trusting God because we believe that there is an infinite grace of God that is available for us. Again, Foster recommends that the petitioner should wait patiently and trust in God, and he describes how we can learn to stay neutral while learning to wait patiently. Here, we can encourage ourselves by saying "I do not understand what is happening and I know that I am in the wilderness, but one thing is sure I do know that the desert will give way to the land flowing with meek and honey." Thus, we come to the realization that God is our hope and we allow our profoundest grieve to call out to the deep infinite love of God to save us.

Furthermore, the next type of prayer that Foster talks about is the *unceasing prayer.* Here, the petitioner is committed to unceasing invocation of the name of God. Also, we move into this way of life through practice and we become unceasing centered and focused. We find we go through our daily activity easily became we are focus on God. The most important effect of this practice is that it helps us grow spiritually and it helps us develop deep intimacy with God through regular association.

Thus, Foster calls this kind of practice, a "Holy habit" because here the believer begins to develop a deep reliance on God as Jesus himself told his disciple to abide in the father so that the father may abide in you.[70] In addition, there are two parts of unceasing prayer that Foster highlighted in his book. The most popular one that is well known among theologians is called "breath prayer." Thus, this concept arose from the idea that we make a petition that can be spoken in one breath. An example of this kind of prayer is the Jesus prayer "Lord Jesus Son of God, have mercy upon me a sinner." It is important to note that breath prayers are requests and not self-centered prayers, but an act of ceaseless reflection on the will of God. Also, Foster speaks about the "practice of presence" as an act of being present to the spirit of God, spending time in his presence. For me, I like this aspect of the book because it reminds me of my personal spiritual practice of praying ceaselessly. Thus, by adopting a spiritual practice of engaging in a continuous prayer habit, I have found that this way of living draws me closer to God to the extent that I am always reminded of his grace towards my life. Also, I have found this practice brings joy and fulfillment constantly to my mind because I have noticed that if I do not pray I cannot function in my daily activity. For me, prayer has come to be like the breath that sustains my life. It has opened my mind to be aware of God's glory in the world. For instance, during my regular Sunday evening walk, I try to pray as I walk and at the end of my walk I seat down calmly close to a fortune lake. Also, as I sat down I turn on my phone to listen to soft Christian music and all I do is to gaze continuously at the flow of the water coming out of the fountain. My reason for choosing to follow up with this habit weekly is that by stopping and gazing at the fountain I want to keep my mind in the present and be aware of his presence as I focus on the beauty of creation. Amazingly, right there I can see the colors of the sky reflecting on the water as it falls back into the lake, I can see birds flying, ducks stopping

---

70 NIV

to drink water and I can see male and female lovers holding hands and snugging each other for me this is the beauty of God in creation.

The fifth prayer that Foster talks about is the *meditation prayer.* Foster describes this kind of prayer as the tongue of the soul and the language of our prayer. Meditation moves from the mouth to the heart. According to Foster the truth being produced by the mouth is regurgitated into the heart. Also, Foster points out to his readers that the key to meditation is the openness of the heart to God. In addition, when it comes to meditation we are bound to scripture and devotional writing. In meditation, we must be filled with the scripture before we can enter into the holies. Thus, Foster encourages his reader to create the conditions that will help the heart to be open to God. One of such ways we can do this is by reading the scripture and listen to what God was saying. For example, we can take a single word and let it reside in us. Also, in mediation, the imagination of the meditator has to be sanctified. Foster explained this kind of sanctification as an act of picturing what the meditator wants to see and what he desires. Thus, in meditation on the scripture, we have to picture the words that we are meditating on and we do this to the extent that it becomes a part of our sub-consciousness that we can visualize what we are saying. Also, apart from meditating on the scripture, there are other sources of sacred text that we can also use for meditational prayers. A good example is *Lectio Divina.* Thus, in this kind of reading the head is drawn to the heart and they are both connected to God. Here, we are seeking the word exposed to the text and the word is Christ. Again, Foster sees it very useful for believers to share from the works of holy men and women of all ages.

Furthermore, the next prayer that Foster talks about is *praying the ordinary.* To pray the ordinary means turning our ordinary experience of life as prayer. First, we are turning our experience to prayer; next, we pray our experiences to God. Lastly, we turn the ordinary to God. Here, we noticed that there is an interdependence and interrelationship between the sacred and the non-sacred. Also, here the common and the ordinary are sanctified in such a way that our everyday normal life becomes treated and seen as something sacred. Foster describes this as the unspeakable holiness in all things. An example of this is our treating our vocational life as an act of prayer. According to Foster "all vacationists are praying by offering his or her work to God. Here, it is important to realize that God is present even in the most meaningless jobs. Following this point, the next type of prayer that Foster talks about is the *prayer of action*. Here, every action performed within the will of God and in the mind of God is a prayer. Therefore, it means that each activity of our daily life is a prayer. For example, any time we offer ourselves to help out someone in need it simply means that we are praying. In addition, Foster sees the praying the ordinary prayer as being necessary practice to have in every Christian home. Some suggestions that he gave was having what he calls the family altar or creating a sacred space in the family home where we can always go whenever we want to pray. Again, I resonate with the importance of this having a sacred space because as part of my family tradition in our home my mum has always made out a sacred sport of prayer and I try to have one in my room where I always go to pray at every prayer time. Also, another form of prayer that Foster speaks about is called the *Healing prayer* here; God's greatest gift is manifested during healing prayers. Thus, in this type of prayer we bring our soul, body, faith and emotion, will and mind under the power of the Holy Spirit so that God can manifest his incarnation power. Also, Foster encourages his readers to pray for healing and restoration always, and even when the sickness or pain does not go away we should not enter into the blame syndrome, but rather when praying for people we should always believe that God in his infinite mercy will hear us and we should be humble enough to wait patiently. The key here is to start from a compassionate point like Jesus did reaching out to the person in need and then allowing God to do the healing himself. Also, there are two steps that Foster suggested that are vital in this type of prayer these are: the petitioner has to listen to what God is saying about the situation and he/she has to ask

God what he should do or how he/she should pray. Next, he/she has to believe that the request has been granted, and lastly he/she should give thanks to God for the healing received. In conclusion, the last type of prayer that Foster talks about is the called *Radical Prayer*. He defined radical prayer as the total transformation of person, people, and institution. Also, in radical prayer, there is a belief that something can be done differently and that something will change instantly. This kind of prayer helps us to develop what Foster called "Holy boldness" this is when we come to God asking Him for forgiveness of our sins, sins of our neighbor, and sins of the nation. Here, we are willing to take on the situation heads on without flinching not because we are insane or acting foolishly but because we trust in God's faithfulness.

5.3.5 EXERCISE 12

To sharpen your skill in analyzing and evaluating the content of a text by way of critically reflecting on your experience, retuning to events in your life that can apply the ideas of the book or that you may not apply same.

1. Does this text challenge you to rethink your belief, relationship, and practices in any way? Do you find yourself agreeing with the author by responding yes?
2. Does this new experience call for a change or modification of the relationship with people in your network?
3. Are you aware of the risks involved in adapting my faith by rationalizing and holding back from being judgmental?

6.1 BOOK REVIEW READING TOOL

Christ and Culture, H. Richard Niebuhr, Harper Collins, New York, 1996.

How to Think Theologically, Howard W. Stone and James O. Duke. Fortress Press, Minneapolis, 2013.

The Pursuit of God. A.W. Tozer. Michigan, Baker Publishing Group, 2013

Life of the Beloved: Spiritual Living in a secular world, Henri J.M. Nouwen. New York, Crossroad Publishing Company, 1992.

Practical Theology: An Introduction, Richard R. Osmer. Michigan, William B Eerdmans, 2008.

Why Do Men Barbecue?: Recipes for Cultural Psychology. Richard A. Shweder. Cambridge, MA: Harvard University Press, 2003.

The McDonaldization of Society, George Ritzer, SAGE publications, Maryland, 2013.

Spiritual Preparation for Christian Leadership, E. Glenn Hinson, Upper-Room Books, Nashville, 1999.

An Altar in the World: A Geography of Faith, Barbara Brown Taylor, HarperCollins, New York, 2010.

Pastoral Theology: Essentials of Ministry, Oden, and Thomas. New York: Harper One, 1983.

For All the Saints: Evangelical Theology and Christian Spirituality, Timothy George & Alister McGrath, Westminster John Knox Press, Louisville, 2003.

Prayer: Finding the Hearts True Home, Richard Foster. HarperCollins, San Francisco, 1992.